Content Marketing

Growth Strategies to Stay Ahead in the Changing World of Content Marketing and Maximize ROI.

Author: Ralf Percy

© Copyright 2020 - All rights reserved.

The content contained within this book may not be reproduced, duplicated or transmitted without direct written permission from the author or the publisher.

Under no circumstances will any blame or legal responsibility be held against the publisher, or author, for any damages, reparation, or monetary loss due to the information contained within this book, either directly or indirectly.

Legal Notice:

This book is copyright protected. This book is only for personal use. You cannot amend, distribute, sell, use, quote or paraphrase any part, or the content within this book, without the consent of the author or publisher.

Disclaimer Notice:

Please note the information contained within this document is for educational and entertainment purposes only. All effort has been executed to present accurate, up to date, and reliable, complete information. No warranties of any kind are declared or implied. Readers acknowledge that the author is not engaging in the rendering of legal, financial, medical or professional advice. The content within this book has been derived from various sources. Please consult a licensed professional before attempting any techniques outlined in this book.

By reading this document, the reader agrees that under no circumstances is the author responsible for any losses, direct or indirect, which are incurred as a result of the use of information contained within this document, including, but not limited to, — errors, omissions, or inaccuracies.

Free Gift

This book includes a bonus booklet. This giveaway may be for a limited time only. All information on how you can secure your gift right now can be found at the end of this book.

Table of Contents

BOOK DESCRIPTION: 3
INTRODUCTION 5
CHAPTER 1 BUILD AN OPT-IN OFFER 7
   Here are some asset types for compelling opt-in offers: 8
   Build an Onboarding Sequence 9
   Make Sales Offers 13
CHAPTER 2 THE MONEY IS IN THE FOLLOW-UP 18
   The Proactive Dashboard 27
   Key takeaway: What can you stop doing today that isn't generating results? 29
CHAPTER 3 CREATING THE RIGHT CONTENT 33
   Define Your 10x Workflows 36
      Determine When Each Task Should Be Done 41
      Estimate How Long Each Task Should Take 43
   Analyzing Content 46
      How to Create the Best Content on Any Topic on the Internet 47
   Let's look at each step to put it to work in your 10x content. 53
      Step One: Keyword Research 53
      Step Two: Analyze What's Ranking Now 54
      Step Three: 10x the Competition in the Face 55
      How to Use a Content Scorecard 60
CHAPTER 4 WHO ARE YOU WRITING FOR? 66

Why is the Strategy Behind Free Content So Important?................... 67

CHAPTER 5 THE PROFILE OF A COPYWRITER 69

To have a little bit of talent... 69

You love to write 70

Be willing to start at low prices... 70

Be confident about being different.. 70

Be prepared to sell yourself... 71

Be prepared to become a Nazi grammar 71

Develop Patience.. 71

A desire to speak up, with objectivity and humility........................... 72

Strategy and creativity.. 72

Be available to write samples.. 72

Be open to new opportunities.. 73

Write/change a piece of content into a functional one;..................... 73

Sell a product/service 73

Persuade the consumer.. 73

Use different styles of writing... 74

Create Solutions.. 74

Style Formatting 77

The font... 77

Use short paragraphs.. 77

Word Play... 77

Break the Rules 78

Acceptability... 78

CHAPTER 6 CLIENTS WANT PROVEN RESULTS............. 80

The Power of Landing Pages... 82

CHAPTER 7 CONTENT MARKETING FOR FACEBOOK MARKETING.. 97

Facebook Content Marketing..97
Liking..98
Sharing...99
Clicking on links..99
Appeal to people's emotions..99
Use your target user's language and way of speaking..................100
Use words popular on the internet...100
Use the "post description" to catch attention..............................100
Use the power of the red arrow in photos....................................101

CONCLUSION...103
DOWNLOAD YOUR FREE GIFT BELOW:.......................108
CHECK OUT OUR OTHER *AMAZING* TITLES:.............110

Auditing Your Online Presence on Social Media Channels 112
Know Your Customers' Tastes and Preferences 114
A Mission Statement That Defines Your Brand...................................... 117
Blogs: What Are They?.. 130
How Does a Blog Help Your Brand?... 130
Blogs as Your Social Media Center 133

These 14 New Habits Will Double Your Income, from Today

An Easy Cheat Sheet to Adopting 14 Powerful Success Habits:

Stop Procrastinating and Start Earning with Intent Now!

Are Your Bad Habits Keeping You from the Life You Want?

Mine definitely were, but then I dedicated myself to *new habits* – and everything changed!

Most people get stuck in same old routines. We eat the same breakfast, we talk to the same people. Human beings are creatures of habit, and it locks us into negative cycles we don't even know are there. Like me, you've had enough of the same-old, same-old. It's time for change!

This guide gives you the 14 most high impact habits that helped me double my income nearly instantly, when I set out on this journey. I will help you change, and I'll make it stick!

Ralf Percy

This FREE Cheat Sheet contains:

- Daily success habits that the most successful people in the world live by

- Common, but little-known habits that will surprise you

- Details on what Stephen Covey, Oprah Winfrey, Elon Musk, Bill Gates and Albert Einstein did that you aren't doing to maximize your earning potential

- Tips on how to overcome habit fatigue

- The reality of adopting difficult, challenging habits and the rewards that result

Scroll below and click the link to claim your cheat sheet!

It's tough to admit that you're doing it wrong. I went through it, and it sucks. After that I was free to change however necessary, to meet my goals. I want you to know that change is waiting for you. This guide is so easy to follow, and if you put it to work in your life – you will double your income.

Adopt these habits, and change your life.

CLICK HERE!!

Book Description:

Do you want to kick-off your successful content marketing business? As a writer, you can enter the lucrative world of content marketing and secure a successful, high-income career.

Writers used to earn pennies. Today, everyone needs good writing. It's a commodity that has made content marketers high in demand. If you can learn how to create content that performs for your clients, you'll never be without work again. Better yet, you'll earn more than doctors do!

In *Content Marketing*, I will teach you the system that will take you from zero to high flyer in the world of content marketing. Learn to apply your writing skills in the marketing arena, and you will be amazed at the results you can get. This is the career you've been waiting for!

In this step-by-step guide you'll learn:

- How exactly to build an amazing opt-in offer
- Where the money is and how to get it
- How to create the right content, then 10X your results
- To understand what it takes to be a great copywriter
- How to build fantastic landing pages that sell things like hot cakes

- How to market content on Facebook for wider reach

With this all-in-one get-started guide, you'll unpack the most direct route to becoming a competent, in-demand content marketing writer – in just a few days.

Get into content marketing when you apply the tried and tested tips in this guide. There's no time like right now to begin your new, lucrative career!

Become a content marketing superstar with this easy guide.

Buy it now and start writing!

Introduction

"In the middle of every difficulty lies opportunity."

– Albert Einstein

Many businesspeople underplay the role of content marketing in their marketing strategy. This can be a costly error. The message is at the core of any good marketing campaign; understand the way that prospects read their email and you can create a message that will gain and hold their attention, boosting response rates to new levels.

With a little inside knowledge and a little work, you can make a major impact on the income you can generate from your list.

Let's say you have a list of 1,000 subscribers and are currently converting on your email at a rate of 3%. You're getting 20 interested customers. If 50% of them buy a product that nets you $45, then you have made $675. Now imagine that you have adjusted your email marketing copy and bump that conversion rate to 8%. Given the same scenario, you have made $1,800! If you just move that conversion rate up 2 percentage points to 5%, you still boost your income by $450 in that scenario.

Use the 50 tips in this report to fine-tune your email content marketing skills to make your customers/prospects/subscribers more loyal and responsive, and your marketing list more profitable.

Your content doesn't have to be long, it doesn't have to have glossy post-production, or be overly complicated. It *does* need to be interesting and useful, and it *does* have to be engaging and visible. The content you produce should give away the farm. Don't hold anything back from your audience; let them see exactly how you do business, what your processes and perspectives are, and show them that you're a real authority by sharing everything you know.

This book comes with a FREE Bonus chapter section as a gift. You can download them for free. The free content can be found at the bottom of this book.

Chapter 1
Build an Opt-In Offer

"Success is walking from failure to failure with no loss of enthusiasm."

– Winston Churchill

If you spend much time online, particularly in internet marketing circles, you can't avoid hearing about the 'powers' of content marketing. To hear some people talk about it, you would think they'd found the fountain of youth and a vault full of money right beside it… but content on its own is just not enough. Yes, it's powerful because it can cut through the noise online and show your visitors that you can be trusted. But if you're going to build a relationship with those visitors, you've got to have a way to continue communicating with them regularly. You can't assume they'll remember to check your blog every week or that they'll buy from you unprompted.

Most content is distributed on platforms you do not own — Facebook, Twitter, content networks, search engines, and so on. Those platforms own the traffic, and if they change how they do business, you can lose your audience. That's why it's critical to start building a contact list that you own and can market to directly. This is where opt-in offers come into play. Whenever a new person visits your site, they should have the opportunity to join your mailing list or private community in exchange for some incentive. You need to get their email address or have them set up an account so that you can build up a profile for them over time, communicate with them directly, and make carefully targeted sales offers to them when the time is right.

Your opt-in offers do not need to be cripplingly complex. This is a critical aspect of a content marketing strategy, so let me be clear: done is better than perfect. Assets like this can always be more detailed, have a longer word-count, or be more testimonial-heavier, but once you have a good piece of information that's useful, polished and appealing, publish it. Every day that you do not have an active opt-in is a day that you are losing leads, and are wasting the resources you've put into creating your content so far. Ideally, you would give the subscriber a piece of premium content, but at the very least, a pop-up box that asks for their email address will do (use SumoMe.com to get that set up).

Here are some asset types for compelling opt-in offers:

- Industry report or white paper

- Case study

- Video series

- Webinar

- Demo

- Discount code

- Quiz or survey

- Cheat sheet

- How-to guide

- Industry or client profiles

Pick the type of asset most appropriate to your industry, and based on what your customers will value. Make sure that it's better information than they would usually find within your public content, and make it feel high-quality wherever possible so that they're impressed and want to see what comes next. The offer should also have a clear benefit for the subscriber: take care to communicate the value they are going to get as a result of giving you their information, and that you set their expectations accurately before they opt in. Make sure the asset is delivered to them immediately, via a thank-you page and/or a confirmation email.

Build an Onboarding Sequence

Getting someone's email address or having them create an account is a big win. This is a micro-commitment from them (which is the first step towards having them buy from you), as well as getting their permission to market to them. This is huge, and you want to capitalize on this opportunity. An email onboarding sequence creates a window for you to do that. Onboarding, also referred to as 'organizational socialization', is done through an automated sequence of emails by which subscribers are educated about your brand, engaged with your community, and indoctrinated with your values.

Here's a templated structure you can use for a general onboarding sequence. If someone has opted in to receive something, these are some general topics for the emails you might send them:

(We'll go into further depth on how to build your onboarding sequences later on in this book.)

The goal of this sequence is to establish yourself as an authority on the topic they opted in to hear about and to get them to take the next step with you. Whether it's booking a call, taking a demo, joining a webinar, or even just replying to an email, make sure you're positioning the subscriber to engage. This is mission-critical. People need to be led, so make sure you have something specific you are leading them towards. You never want someone to be unclear about what their next step should be. This is true at any point as the customer is moving through your ecosystem, but *particularly* at this stage when they've been exposed to your ideas and expertise, and it's time for them to make a purchasing decision.

Depending on the nature of your market, your offering, and the messaging that works best, common 'next steps' in a B2B business would be one of the following:

- Invite them to a free webinar. A lot of marketers do this extremely well — people like Frank Kern, Noah Kagan, and Ryan Levesque leverage webinars to engage people to great success all the time. This format works so well because it allows the marketer to give a lot of value up front, without requiring a large time investment from the prospect. Webinars are also a direct platform to sell from, as they basically create a captive audience: the prospect joins the webinar, learns lots of good stuff, and then (with the principle of reciprocity working quietly in the back of their mind) will sit through a sales pitch even if they don't have to. At this point, the prospect is primed: they think of you as an approachable authority who is speaking directly to their problems, and so you can offer them your solution while they are right there in a receptive frame of mind.

- Offer them a free demo. This works similar to the webinar model but works particularly well for SaaS (software as a service) businesses and companies that offer some kind of technical solution.

We built a free demo offer into the onboarding email sequence for Wicked Reports, and they saw a significant uptick in both booked demos and sales. Having some prior education about the product, their prospects become very curious to see the tool in action in a few different scenarios, and are therefore willing to book in an hour to get to know Wicked Reports better. Most people learn well in a visual format, so seeing the tool in use is a powerful way to move them towards a conversion. Do you know the old saying "possession is nine-tenths of the law"? Well, an interactive demo is about as close as you can get to having the prospect 'possess' the product. If you can demonstrate your offer in action, they're going to be much more likely to take the next step you want.

- Invite them to a free call. This works particularly well for consultants and service businesses because often the offer is a little less tangible than what's being sold by other B2B businesses. Make it clear that it's an obligation-free call, and that they can spend as much time as they want to ask questions, picking apart your offer, and really getting a feel for whether you're the right fit for them. It's an opportunity for them to air any skepticism, get clarity about what they need, and get to know you. A very powerful part of the onboarding process is that they get sufficiently educated about your product or process so that they feel comfortable getting on the phone with you because they will then know what they're talking about. You never want someone to come into a conversation this blind, because the power balance is too much in your favor. In that situation, the prospect can feel that you hold all the cards and they don't have enough information to assess whether you're being straightforward with them. This makes people feel defensive, and wary of you trying to 'put it over them'. You want to make sure they have a locus of control in the interaction so that they're comfortable and more open to the conversation. Before getting on the phone with anyone, make sure they have as much information as they need, and let them know that you encourage a critical approach in your customers, that you only want to work with people who take their business seriously, and that you're not going to put a hard sell on them.

All the content that you produce up to this point should be driving the prospect towards having some kind of real-time interaction with you. Business is about people, and people won't do anything if trust and rapport is missing from an interaction. They need to relate to you as a person they can trust; a person who will be a positive influence in their business, and will ultimately help them fill whatever deep-seated need is driving them.

(And make no mistake — it's rarely a cut and dry desire to make more money that drives people. Some want status, others want recognition, others still want positive feedback... there's a whole neurochemical chain reaction going on when someone makes a buying decision, and while that's beyond the scope of this book, we'll be getting into a little bit of the behavioral psychology that should factor into your marketing later on.)

Carlos Ruiz Zafón, one of the most popular Spanish novelists of the modern age, says that we only accept as true what can be narrated. Knowing, then, that people will only buy what you're selling when it's wrapped up in a story or narrative that resonates with them - you need to find a way to position your content in a way that does that. Your offer should be presented as a story they can see themselves taking an active part in, and you, yourself should be presented as a narrator they trust and find relatable.

Understanding that, you should always be driving them to some sort of interactive action. This is a critical aspect of high-converting content: there's always a clear call to action that moves them further through your funnel. The prospect is never left alone without a clear next step; they'll never wonder if you have some hidden ulterior motive — they know and trust you because you told them the story they needed to hear. This is why knowing deeply who your audience is, what offer they need to receive, and how to position your messaging, is the cornerstone of creating high-converting content.

Next, we're going to dive into the two most critical steps of all — making sales offers and following up with your prospects.

Make Sales Offers

The secret to creating content that converts is to create a conversion moment. Yes, despite all the progress that marketing has made, you still have to make sales offers if you want to convert your prospects. No marketing system in the world can extract a sale without first making a sales offer.

All businesses live and die by the number of sales they make. It doesn't matter how good your systems are, or if you have a great team, or you've got unrivalled SOPs... it doesn't even matter if you have hyper-focused marketing and a replicable lead acquisition funnel. If you don't make sales offers, it's all for nothing.

Of the dozens of B2B businesses I've worked with over the years, just one thing separates the success stories from the failures, and it's that the leaders of the company committed to sales. They committed to making the offer every time — they committed to ignoring their fear of rejection, their anxiety about pissing people off, and the voice in their head that said they couldn't do it. They committed, consistently made their offers, and came out on top because of it.

Sales offers come in all shapes and sizes, depending on the business. You might invite someone to book a paid consult with you, or you might offer them an ongoing service for which they pay you every month. You might offer them the purchase of a single unit, or the purchase of thousands of units. You might offer them paid access to a piece of software that will automate part of their business. Whatever it is, you need to explicitly offer to give them your product or service in return for a specific amount of money.

If you are afraid of making sales offers off the back of your content, or you 'sell from your heels' (making a half-hearted attempt at a sale that doesn't really showcase the benefits, or ask the prospect for an answer), your content will never convert a single customer. You will be wasting all your resources and in time, your business will fail.

- Being 'uncovered' as a fraud

- Being rejected

- Being found lacking in either their qualifications or what they're offering

- Being perceived as pushy, rude, or mercenary

- Being unable to deliver what they are offering

Usually, these fears are completely unfounded, and they're all rooted in the fundamental human need to be accepted by your tribe. It's horrible to think that someone you pitch would be offended by your offer, and then go and rip on you all over the internet… but with a content ecosystem that gradually entices people to your offer, and sharing information that benefits them and shows that you have their best interests in mind, you're not going to get that kind of treatment.

The great thing about the content ecosystem is that most of the people you will speak to will be pre-qualified as a potential buyer, so they're likely to respond positively to an offer. The best approach, in this case, is usually not a hard sell, but a simple mention of 'here's what I've got, here's what it will do for you, and here's how to get it.'

In fact, I've never had a client have a bad reaction from their customers when they make their sales offer at the end of a content funnel. I've never had a bad reaction for my own services, either. That doesn't mean bad reactions can't happen — selling is both art and science, and you *can* get it wrong, but if you are putting your customers first then you can feel confident that you'll usually get a good response.

If need be, practice your sales offers. Get a friend or colleague on the phone, or in however method you will be making pitches to customers, and practice on them. It's worth the awkwardness and will pay a huge ROI on the time and energy you spend on it. Ideally, your practice partner will actually fit your primary customer profile. Give them your onboarding material to read first, so that they come to the practice sales situation with all the same knowledge your real prospects will have. Go through the process of the onboarding event — whether it's a webinar, demo or call — and then transition into your sales offer.

Practice moving the conversation from the free content to the sales offer. Practice your positioning, and how you talk about the offer. Practice the language that works best to communicate all the benefits of the offer, and practice how to overcome objections by encouraging your partner to come up with as many as they can, based on what you've already discussed. Finally, find out from them what questions went unanswered for them during the process, what objections they kept to themselves, and what would have made them commit to the sale that you didn't address. Try to get a real-world interaction that will emulate the sales process for you, so that when you do it with real prospects, you're in familiar territory.

Never pass up the opportunity to make a sale. If you have someone on a call, or in some kind of interaction with you, do not put it off. Do not say to yourself *"I'll just send them an email that closes them after this"* or *'they'll tell me if they want to go ahead with something"*. No, you won't, and no, they won't. Unless you have explicitly promised not to sell them anything, always be selling.

(The only time you should ever promise not to sell during an interaction is when you need something from the prospect other than the sale, like early market feedback. Otherwise, avoid making promises that will prevent you from making money.)

Be as generous and fully present as you can be during the sales process. Answer every question honestly and with your full attention. Dig into their doubts, invite them to hit you with their best shot — make them understand that you *really* care about their situation and are helping them to find the right solution. Before they get off the call, get a yes or no answer from the prospect. Just ask: *"Are you ready to go ahead?"* No maybes, or let-me-think-about-its. Yes or no. If they push back on you, simply say that you want to get a specific answer from them so you know how to move forward with them. It might sound aggressive, but when positioned correctly, this is a powerful method to make sure that all the content you've produced so far actually does the job and makes people convert.

Chapter 2
The Money Is in The Follow-Up

"The most unprofitable item ever manufactured is an excuse."

– John Mason

This is the most important principle you can learn in marketing. It's rare that a visitor will convert on their first visit to your site, or that even a warm prospect will convert at their first point of contact with you. Of course, if your initial onboarding funnel does a great job of orienting them into your business and demonstrating your value, you might have a pretty good conversion rate right out of the gate. But for most companies (particularly those making high price-point offers) getting the conversion can take a few interactions. People want to get to know the way you approach the industry, that you're a trustworthy and legitimate company, and that other people have successfully done business with you.

Now, assuming that your prospects have gone through each part of the ecosystem, they should know, like, and trust you. They should understand the benefits of what you're offering, and they should understand your perspective on the industry. If they haven't bought from you yet, then it's time to bring a follow-up system to life so that all your hard work helps get them past the tipping point, rather than indefinitely hovering around it.

Content Marketing

If someone says no when you make your sales offer, here's what you do. You tell them that you are going to send them a recap of your conversation, so that they can reply with any questions that come to them afterwards, and that you're going to follow up with them in a few weeks (and make sure it goes on your calendar to do so). When you follow up with them as promised, you'll often find that they have made no progress towards their stated goals. This is where you can restate their exact motivation for speaking with you and highlight how you can help them: *"Here's the offer I made you last time. Here's the way I can make it even better for you, so you can stop wasting time and start seeing the progress you need: [insert offer here of a discount, done-for-you element, additional features, bonuses, etc]."*

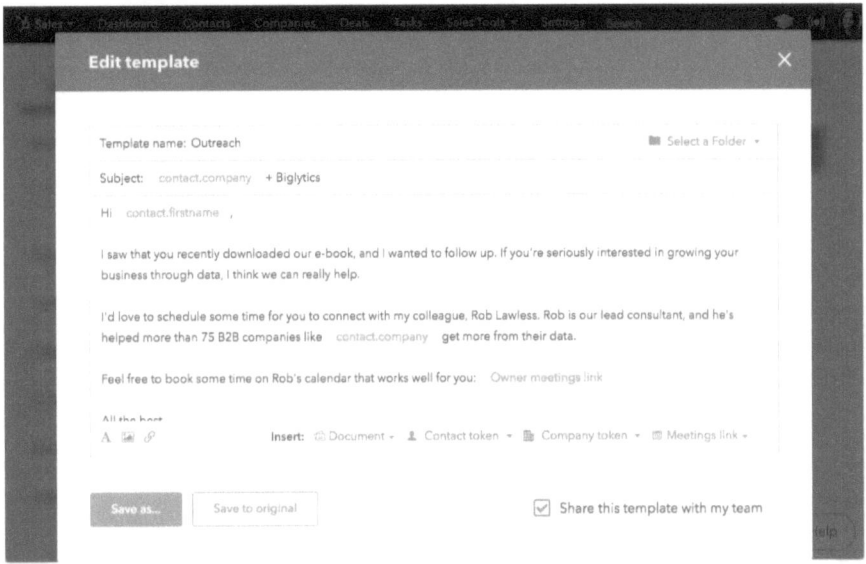

Figure 1.

Alternately, if you would rather automate your follow-up, you can build out two email funnels to do all this work for you: one funnel for people who converted, and one for people who have not converted yet, using the same process you used to build your onboarding email funnel. The funnel for people who do convert should include welcome material, next steps for them to get started with you, and bonus content. For people who have not converted yet, provide more educational and useful content, and keep inviting them to conversion opportunities.

Figure 2.

Content assets are long-form pieces of content that you can use to attract high-end clients, by demonstrating that you are an authority and that you have an uncommon depth of knowledge in your industry. Sharing your expertise in a generous, transparent way like this is a powerful way to get your business in front of big clients who could change the game for you. In your content asset, you really pull back the curtain on your expertise, writing the playbook on how your clients could implement your custom strategies to solve their problems.

It sounds like giving away your secret sauce, but in reality, people just want to taste the sauce and know how you make it, rather than making the sauce themselves. The ingredients for Sriracha Hot Sauce are listed in detail on Wikipedia, but no one wants to make it themselves. They want to buy that bottle with the rooster on it and have it ready to go without having to find all the specialty grocers, get the right balance of ingredients, and then sweat it out in the kitchen themselves. It's the same with your process: people are curious about the details, but they really just want the result without having to do the work themselves.

ViperChill is just one business that provides a great example of this. The owner, Glen Allsopp, regularly produces incredibly valuable long-form content about SEO on his blog. He doesn't withhold any key information or force you to opt-in to get this content. He shares everything that's been working for his selection of SEO-drive niche websites, big upcoming opportunities in the industry, as well as transparent updates about the progress of his business. Far from costing him work, Glen gets to be totally selective about his client roster — his expertise and generosity show that he's the best in the business, and so the best in *other* businesses line up to work with him.

The big win, of course, is that pulling back the curtain like this makes you look like a giant. It implies that it doesn't matter to you if people do it themselves, or even if your competitors steal your system — your business is so robust and you have so much confidence in your process that you can easily afford for that to happen. It's an attractive attitude to clients who want to work with the best in the field.

The most common content assets used in B2B businesses are books and training courses. Any large piece of content you create that will hold its value and separate you from the market is a content asset. I'm going to use books as my key example throughout this section, as that's what I specialize in, but all this information applies just as well to training courses and other long-form assets.

Creating a content asset and building a strategy around it is not the right move for all businesses. E-commerce companies, for example, are generally better served by recurring content. Businesses with low price-point products also do better with recurring content — there's a much lower barrier to purchase among the audience, and creating a long-form asset may be overkill. But if your business sells high-ticket items or services, then a content asset is a powerful demonstration of authority and credibility. It can shortcut the process of winning trust and confidence from potential clients and is an incomparable differentiator from your competitors.

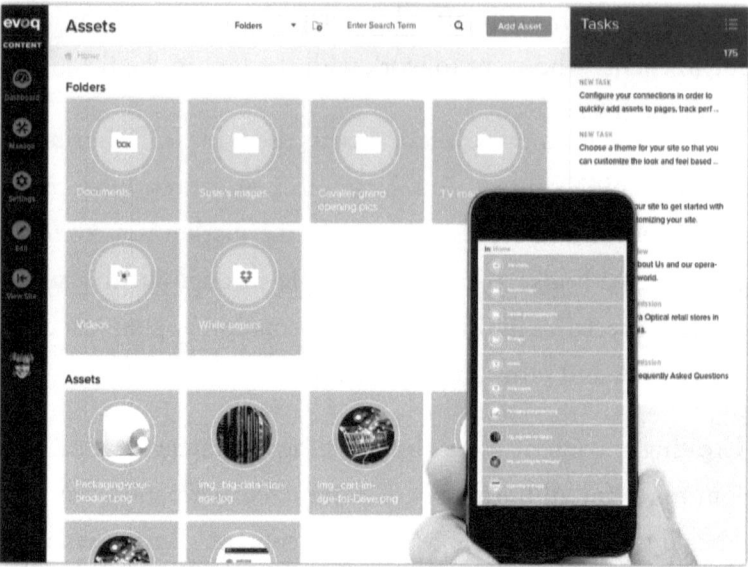

Figure 3.

It requires a massive effort to build this kind of content asset. If you are running your own business, finding the time to write every day is going to be tough — particularly to get to the kind of word count that makes publishing a book worthwhile. And once you decide to write a book, speed to market becomes important, so that you're not beaten to the punch by a competitor with the same idea.

All the people for whom I've ghostwritten books have been met with this exact problem: they have too much to do in their businesses to make real progress on their book each day. They realize that if it's going to happen, someone else needs to take the lead. Where they can produce 300 or 500 words a day, a good professional writer can produce 3000 to 5000 words a day… and when you're writing a book with a 40,000 or 50,000-word count, the difference in timeline is massive.

Content Marketing

What usually decides it for them, though, is that the book needs to be marketed *at the same time* it is being written. If you are going to create real momentum for your business with your book, it needs to launch to fanfare and blanket coverage where your primary customers are going to see it (not to launch to crickets and then slowly build up a following over time). The business owner has the connections and positioning to make that happen, but they can't do that and write the damn thing at the same time. They hand the legwork off to me and then focus instead on getting it in front of the right people. Even if you have a dedicated audience who will be supportive, you want to be seeding their interest, getting early purchasing commitments from them, and having them commit to sharing it for you when the time comes.

That element — getting it in front of the right people — is the most critical part of producing a content asset. You want to use it to attract higher value customers, and as a way to 'rack the shotgun' to get the attention of people who are serious about solving the problem you specialize in. The people who are willing to read a book about your solution are often going to be the same people who are willing to pay an expert to take care of it for them — when you're thinking about creating an asset like this, you need to think of it with your future sales system in mind.

Content hackers can always change their minds, but the marketing-plan mindset is inflexible because it lives and dies by the words, charts, and mission statements chiseled on those fifty-two sheets of paper.

For the marketing-plan marketer, once you make the plan, you work it. That's not how it works for the content hacker. And if you suitably increase your tolerance for failure, you're ready to put unheard-of methodologies to work for you - the things that "just aren't done!" This is how you can 10x your business—and in short order.

What will content hacking look like for you?

Figure 4.

10x Marketing Interview: Noah Kagan and the Proactive Dashboard

Content hacking forces you to innovate and take risks because there are such high-potential rewards. However, with innovation and risk comes failure - and lots of it.

The Proactive Dashboard

According to Noah, most of your growth attempts aren't going to work. This is why he's adopted a framework for growth that systematically tests ideas, keeping the winners and chucking the duds. His team at Sumo documents does these tests using what they call proactive dashboards.

Each week, their teams test a fresh idea and track its results on their dashboard. That means they test fifty-two new ideas each year. From content to ads to email, they're constantly testing. Noah says the regular routine of testing promotions forces his team to find the stuff that works.

Imagine what that would look like for your company. How innovative would you get if you forced each marketing team—or even team member—to test a never-before-tried method each week? This kind of consistent innovation fosters growth and helps avoid the copycat marketing trap.

Here's the thing, though. In the last four months, only two tests have worked. In fact, 86 percent of Sumo's tests haven't worked. So, if you have more than two out of ten attempts succeed, you're sitting pretty. And rather than be depressing, that statistic should actually be encouraging. Failure is the nature of the beast. But every time you learn what doesn't work, it allows you to kill it and allows room for finding something that does work.

Building Out the Dashboard

To begin, every item on the dashboard has to be fully controllable by you and your team. This means that you cannot be dependent upon anything outside of your activities. The problem is that most of the metrics we're looking at as marketers have already happened. So, this dashboard isn't simply based upon past results you cannot change. It's proactive in that it's filled with goals you can influence right now.

This is a living dashboard that's updated live. Then, as you move forward, you measure against the secondary metric you're hoping to impact. If it doesn't move the needle, you stop doing it. But if it does, it's a keeper.

Noah explains, "We have two proactive dashboards. We have one for Sumo.com and one for each business unit. The idea, and the reason I love them is that everything has to be completely controllable by you. What does that mean? It means you can't be dependent on anything . . . The dashboard is solely the things we have full control of each week. It's a live-tracking, living dashboard."

Sumo has a proactive dashboard for each marketing team. Here's a breakdown of their dashboards for two of their teams, advertising, and content:

Advertising

Advertising has to spend a certain amount, which is completely in their control. This means they can run as many ad variations as they want within their budget. Each week, they spend $7,560 and run at least five variations.

Key Takeaway: What can you directly control and measure in real time?

Content

The content team measures how many pieces of content they publish per week. And on this content, they test things like headlines, email opt-ins, marketing promotion tests, and promotional ad spend. For instance, they tested five weekly posts on Quora for each week. After measuring, however, they saw only 1,000 visitors from each post—which for their team did not merit continuing. The team decided this when they compared it to LinkedIn, which was getting ten times the results Quora was.

Key takeaway: What can you stop doing today that isn't generating results?

Defining and Understanding Your Target Audience

Implicit in the activities of content hacking is a target audience to which you tailor your content. This makes defining and deeply understanding your ideal customer paramount. For Sumo, this was an evolutionary process. As they grew, so did their understanding of who best benefited from their product.

To do this, the Sumo team looked at which customers churn the least, have the highest lifetime value and are easiest for their sales team to talk to and close deals with. They then worked backward from this group, which made their target audience much more obvious.

They noticed that huge publishers like the New York Times were a tough sell. Alternatively, small solo bloggers were also tough because they had such a small budget, and their tiny cash flow made them averse to paying for tools. After some fine-tuning and research, however, they found that e-commerce customers were their sweet spot. Why? Because they could directly achieve ROI in proportion to email list growth. In other words, if they could grow their email list by a factor of ten, they could multiply their customer base in the same way.

For Noah, this changed their entire approach to marketing and content. Originally, their blog was all about getting more traffic - this was a fine goal at the beginning. And for other marketers, it's a perfect metric when traffic correlates to revenue or whatever their goal outcome is. However, even as Sumo's content team tripled their traffic, there was no proportional increase in revenue. So, traffic was disconnected from their primary growth goal.

To course correct, they shifted to a metric of qualified leads—specifically, how many e-commerce customers they were converting when they visited their site. Now the content team is responsible for qualified signups, which means every test is aimed squarely at influencing this number. In short, their success is a combination of continual testing of growth ideas and tailoring all content and activities to a target customer.

Noah's team is driven by results alone. No big long-term plans, and no grand theories. Noah explains:

I don't think I'm a great marketer—and I don't even know if I'm that great at running businesses. I think what I've actually done well is find products that I just love. Then it's my responsibility to tell the right people in the world about it. That's what I do in marketing; I'm not a genius marketer or anything. I just think, 'Oh, that's a cool product. Oh, that person probably needs to know about it. Now, let me do whatever it takes to make that happen.'

I think for other people out there who want to improve their business or marketing acumen, the easiest thing, besides finding a product you love, is to go help people one by one. It's a common misconception I've seen in marketing and in businesses where people think: 'I gotta scale! And I'm gonna spin up all these Facebook ads! And I gotta try to figure out Reddit! Or I gotta do content or PR,' or some other thing.

If you come back and just go one by one, either do live chats, do phone calls, do in person, do a manual service, I think that really helps you understand your customers better, and helps you understand your business better. Long term that'll help you do really well.

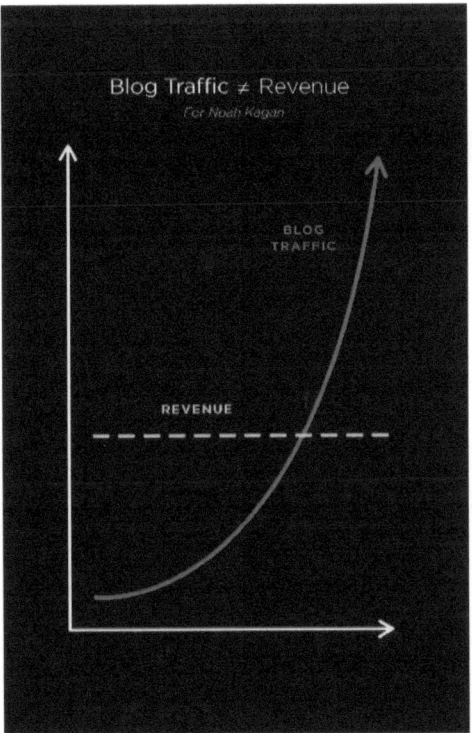

Figure 5.

Noah doesn't claim to know tons about marketing. He doesn't need to, because he knows how to experiment and shift his thinking to follow the results. That's content hacking. And his team exhibits these same traits. They're willing to take risks and then use their reverts when necessary—even if that means using them for 86 percent of their tests.

Three Content Hacks in the Wild

Without a doubt, real-world examples like Noah's are the best way to cement principles into your marketing. So, let's look at three more real-world content hacks. Now, just like everything else so far, they're not intended as a content-marketing buffet for you to choose from. After all, they've already been done. But they are pieces of world-class inspiration you can use to understand the content hacking mindset.

A unique new Business

April 05,2014

Figure 6.

Chapter 3
Creating the Right Content

"Prospecting – find the man with the problem."

– Ben Friedman

At CoSchedule, we recently launched a feature called Marketing Projects. It helps teams manage marketing campaigns. It's a perfect way to drive leads and conversions for our product. However, we use the content core to create valuable content around the core topic.

To do this, we used some good old-fashioned audience research to find two things:

A topic they're highly interested in

An angle that matches their needs

Now, I love tools—after all, our product is a tool. But when it comes to research, I never get too fancy. What I want, and what you should want, too, is to talk directly to your customers. And I think some of the best ways to do this are Google, Facebook, and LinkedIn user groups; email surveys; and simply picking up the phone and making some calls.

What you're looking for are conversations and subtopics around the main topic you'll be covering. In our case, we used Google to research similar content, plus we talked with our customers about their struggles and problems around our new feature. With both tactics, our primary goal was to hear how they described their problems.

First, we found popular blog posts and articles on marketing-project–related topics. Then, we scrolled down to the comments section for each one. Here, we were able to read verbatim questions and comments from people in our target audience. This helped us pick up on the exact phrases they use that were related to our feature, while at the same time helping us more deeply understand their problems and gaps for which there wasn't a current solution.

Second, we talked to our customers. Loaded with the conversational ammo from our initial research, we dug even further into the struggles our current customers faced. We learned they were looking for four primary things:

They needed ways to "organize everything in one place."

They wanted a "marketing schedule template."

They needed help with "marketing campaign planning."

They had gaps in "marketing project management."

From this stage, we were able to tailor our feature launch to these problems perfectly. And we did so with content that fits perfectly into our content core. Not only did we know our audience was interested in the topic; we knew exactly how they explained their needs. And because it was a brand new CoSchedule feature, the angles we chose for our content intersected directly with our business interests.

Content Marketing

Figure 7.

The promise baked into the headline gives the reader the exact benefit as the feature itself. It's also an extremely useful post, clocking in at over 2,500 words, plus free templates to manage and organize marketing projects. And because that value is matched exactly with our feature's value, it converts traffic very well.

Finally, we included a single, clear, and compelling CTA. Here is the in-line body copy and companion graphic:

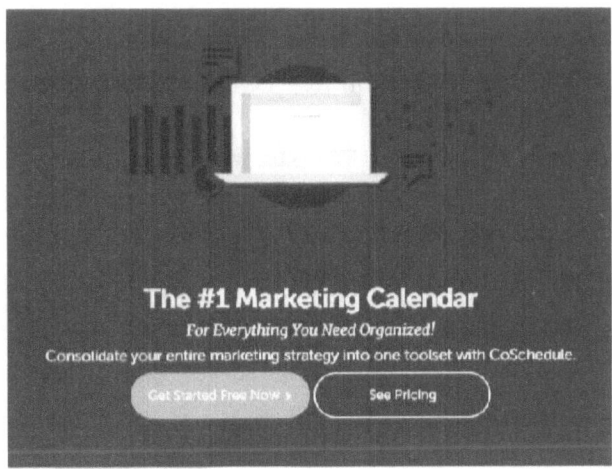

Figure 8.

Define Your 10x Workflows

Your 10x workflows will embody three characteristics. They will: be pre-approved, be lean, and include high standards of performance. Because they're pre-approved, they will reduce rework and needless hang-ups, getting the green light from your boss. Because they're lean, they will include only the essential tasks while being clearly and efficiently organized. And lastly, because they include a high standard of performance, quality won't suffer even though you're able to execute quickly.

When you create your workflows according to the following steps, you will be able to showcase a smartly organized process that will streamline productivity and get consistent results. You'll decrease the friction added by post-work approval processes because you will also limit the number of people involved. The fewer people weighing in on every detail, the faster work ships.

Just like the Oakland A's, your workflows will produce base hit after base hit. Your score will rise steadily inning after inning. Through the relentless execution of the fundamentals, what used to take you seven weeks—or even seven months—can now take just seven days.

Step One: Get Your 10x Workflows Pre-Approved

To start, imagine this scenario: Nathan Ellering, CoSchedule's head of demand generation, found himself in at a former corporate job. He was the manager of their in-house marketing team and invested heavily in content—or, at least he tried to. One of Nathan's main channels was the company blog, which ran on a daily publishing schedule.

This can be a grueling frequency for any marketer to keep up. However, difficulty was compounded by a messy workflow that looked like this:

Get post idea from a subject matter expert (SME)

Assign post to one of the writers

Receive draft from writer

Submit draft to SME for review

Address SME's notes and revise

Re-submit to SME for approval

Receive approval from SME

Submit SME-approved draft to the vice president of marketing for his review

Receive approval (or revisions) from VP

If revisions, edit draft again and re-submit to VP

If no revisions, submit to design

Publish post

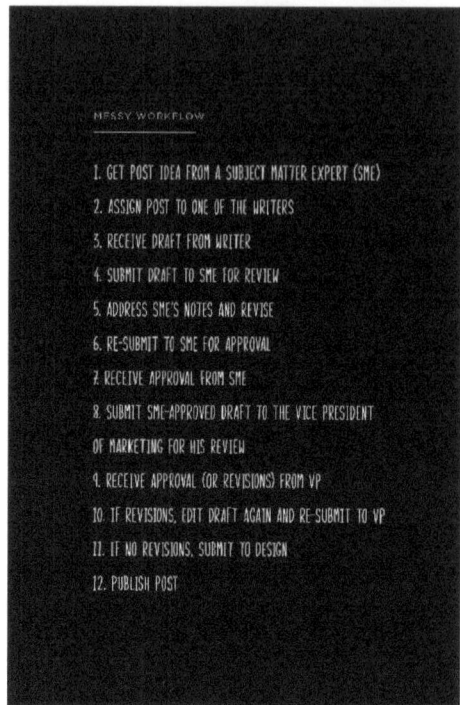

Figure 9.

That's twelve steps involving five people, four levels of bureaucracy, and three layers of approval for each blog post. This meant approvals accounted for 58.3 percent of the total process. That's a lot of approving going on for one blog post.

Instead of being created with a bias toward shipping, testing, and getting results, it was bloated with unnecessary approvals solely in place as a check-your-ass measure. This bureaucratic process existed because one time, someone did something wrong—and this cascaded into wrapping an entire process around failure avoidance. Unnecessary approvals are a poison pill to culture and become huge obstacles to getting the marketing results you were hired to achieve.

If approval-laden processes like the one above sound familiar to you, good news is coming your way: 10x workflows solve this problem immediately. Nathan worked to restructure and fix this process following Step One. The key to streamlining is to reframe expectations. Instead of completing work and then submitting it for approval when completed, you will organize and gain approval on your workflows. Here's the process:

Create the 10x workflow.

Approve the 10x workflow.

Work the 10x workflow.

You will approve the workflow rather than making approval part of the workflow. When approval is part of the process, it becomes the enemy of shipping work quickly. Once you pass things up the ladder, approval will take forever. And you'll be buried in small, 10 percent tweaks because everyone who has a hand in the pie-making process wants to ensure their thumbprints are visible. After all, who wants to submit something to their boss—or their boss's boss—without looking like they've done some work?

If you get your workflows pre-approved, you'll ship faster. In turn, you'll get to 10x results in a fraction of the time. To create your 10x workflows, understand that the simplest approach is the best place to start. Your goal will be to pare down each workflow into its essential components. This process will do exactly that if you follow it closely.

Figure 10.

Here, you will wield the power of batching similar tasks together. In turn, this increases team member productivity by paring down the workload and enhancing focus. However, not only will your team be more productive, they'll be able to move faster than ever. Speed is the result of productivity, and that is what we are after.

As 10x marketers, we are looking to do more with less. If every blog post we publish helps us grow our email list, why not try to find a way to publish twice as much? Or at a minimum, keep the same publishing schedule and ship additional 10x projects? Content hacking, 90 percent good, and the 10x calendar are each dependent on you not only getting things done but doing them so fast your competitors freak.

As you increase your output, 10x workflows will also serve to reduce switching costs. This matters because not only does frequent

Content Marketing

task switching crunch productivity by 40 percent, but it also increases errors. Efficiency is both performing work quickly and doing work well the first time. Thus, you avoid reworking.

According to a 2005 study in the construction industry, rework can add between 7.25 and 12 percent to the direct cost of an entire project. Even if you don't have high overhead costs, your team's time is still worth a great deal—not to mention the project deadlines put at risk. In all, lean workflows will compound their value each time they're performed.

In addition, ensure your tasks are written with a definition of what "done" looks like. This final point of clarity removes ambiguity, reduces back-and-forth, and lets your team know exactly when they're finished. For example, rather than "Write headline and post," the task is labeled, "Write 20–30 headlines + body + proofread." Now the person executing the task understands exactly what the finished product of the task will look like.

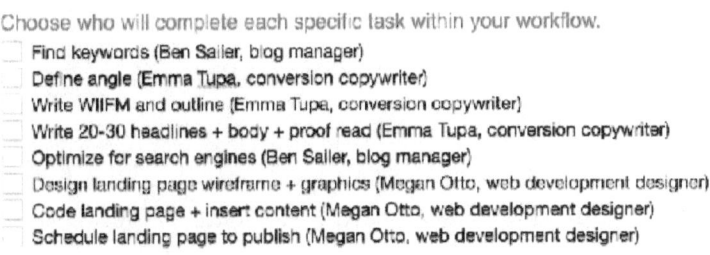

Figure 11.

Determine When Each Task Should Be Done

Generally speaking, most marketers run their content through the process, and once it is done, schedule it for publish. The problem is, this leaves a lot of room for thrashing during that all-too-common 10 percent push. Instead, adopting the content hacker mindset means picking a drop-dead publish date and working backward. Then, execute against that timeline and repeat for every post going forward.

This is what the exercise looks like when applied to CoSchedule's landing page example:

> Determine how many days before publish each task must be completed.
> - [ ] Find keywords (Ben Sailer, blog manager)
>   - 18 days before publish
> - [ ] Define angle (Emma Tupa, conversion copywriter)
>   - 17 days before publish
> - [ ] Write WIIFM and outline (Emma Tupa, conversion copywriter)
>   - 17 days before publish
> - [ ] Write 20-30 headlines + body + proof read (Emma Tupa, conversion copywriter)
>   - 15 days before publish
> - [ ] Optimize for search engines (Ben Sailer, blog manager)
>   - 14 days before publish
> - [ ] Design landing page wireframe + graphics (Megan Otto, web development designer)
>   - 7 days before publish
> - [ ] Code landing page + insert content (Megan Otto, web development designer)
>   - 2 days before publish
> - [ ] Schedule landing page to publish (Megan Otto, web development designer)
>   - 1 day before publish

Figure 12.

For each task for which you create a 10x workflow, you'll notice an immediate bump in efficiency. And the fun part is, this is possible because you're eliminating redundancies and streamlining necessities. Now, who doesn't love doing less work and getting better results?

The goal here is for your team to produce more than ever before. This will happen because of the sweet synergy that happens when 10x workflows are combined with a 10x calendar. Your team will publish more focused content on a regular basis, giving you measurable results.

Estimate How Long Each Task Should Take

Next, we have a small, yet important step. Take a moment to set a limit on how long each task should take. When you do this, your team will understand the level of effort and time they should invest in each task. And, you're able to understand how long the entire workflow should take to accomplish.

Determine how long each task should take.
- ☐ Find keywords (Ben Sailer, blog manager) [30 minutes]
  - 18 days before publish
- ☐ Define angle (Emma Tupa, Conversion copywriter) [15 minutes]
  - 17 days before publish
- ☐ Write WIIFM and outline (Emma Tupa, Conversion copywriter) [60 minutes]
  - 17 days before publish

Figure 13.

These time limits remind me of a phrase used in agile software development regarding scope. Frequently, we will say a portion of a feature is "out of scope" when we are discussing a new development project. This means that before we start building anything, we make a decision about how much time we are willing to dedicate to the feature. The length of the timeline is based on the value the feature will provide the business.

So, if a feature will be only mildly useful to our customers, we may only budget one week for development. This means that our engineers will need to scope that feature to fit the timeline properly. Of course, we will forgo many "nice to have" elements by default, but the reality is that those things were unlikely to result in more value to the business, as we'd already measured the value in terms of one week.

The point is that time limits prevent thrashing, encourage shipping, and enforce the 90 percent good mentality. When you decide 10 percent projects don't matter, you need tight timelines to keep both yourself and your team in check. With this process, your team will immediately know when they are out of scope.

Step Three: Bake a Standard of Performance Directly into Your 10x Workflows

Finally, your workflows will be complete with a standard of performance to guide your team. A standard of performance is exactly what it sounds like - it's the quality and expected outcome of each workflow. This matters because it's a key facet of getting your workflow pre-approved.

The goal is for workflows to produce agreed-upon results. At CoSchedule, the standard of performance for each piece of content we publish is as follows:

Content Core: The topic must be aligned with our content core.

Keyword-driven: The content must be keyword driven for maximum traffic and long-term search performance.

Well-researched: Our content is thoroughly researched so it contains zero fluff and provides facts rather than opinions.

Comprehensive and actionable: The content will cover absolutely everything pertinent for our audience to know: what to do, how to do it, and how to get the results we promise.

Content Marketing

Content upgrade: Every piece of content will have a custom content upgrade that will help our audience do what we're teaching them to do - they can access this in exchange for their email address.

Single, Clear CTA: Finally, every piece of content includes a single, clear, and compelling call-to-action—the content has a job to do, and the CTA is how we close the deal.

Marketers create content to produce results. Content is never the end goal; growth is. When you create your standard of performance, every person involved will understand the results your content (or any workflow you create) is executed to achieve.

In the next chapter, we're going to go deeper into our standards of performance for content. But it's paramount that whatever work you and your team are doing, you understand the results you're supposed to achieve.

Why Are Workflows 10x?

The core of 10x marketing doesn't equal haphazard and disorganized activity. Sometimes, this is the perception of the startup culture ethos. However, the 10x Marketing Formula is firmly rooted in this premise: people work faster, better, and more consistently by creating repeatable processes that consistently produce big results on a dime. This is all about focus and discipline.

In many ways, it's similar to the 10x ideas brainstorming process. There is a time for strategy and a time for creation. There is also a time to develop process strategy—affectionately dubbed 10x workflows. And by compartmentalizing these processes, you can create an efficient, 10x producing machine.

The relentless execution of the fundamentals, getting base hit after base hit, wins ball games. And more importantly, it wins championships, too. So, when you approach crafting your 10x workflows, just envision the Cubs' epic Game 7 World Series win. It was a 10x moment, and the same moments are waiting for you.

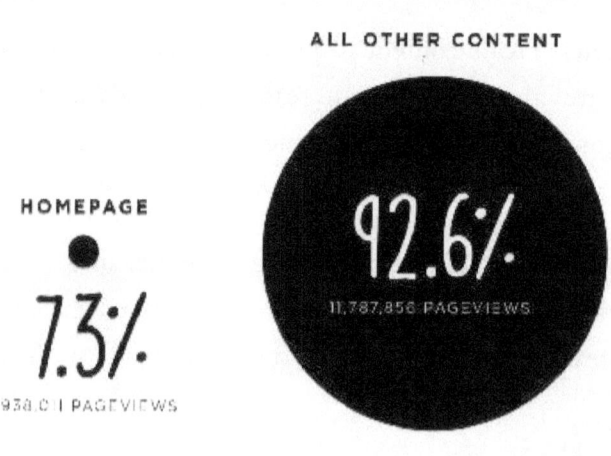

Figure 14.

We all say we aim to produce high-quality content, yet few of us actually write down what that means. If you simply become one of the few that write it down, you can stand out from the crowd. You need a way to execute higher quality, competition-free content, without having to go past the 90 percent good mark. All of this works together and is an absolute must.

Analyzing Content

Like Jeff, we analyzed our content to trace the patterns of which content drove results and which didn't. To do this, we looked at the last fifty blog posts we'd published. At the time, getting unique page views were the 10x metric we were optimizing for. So, out of those fifty posts, we read the top ten with the highest unique pageviews, and then read the bottom ten with the lowest unique pageviews.

As we did, it became quickly evident what qualities were reflected in these top performers. Because we compared them to each other, we found the qualities present in the best performers. And notably, those same qualities were either absent or underdeveloped in the ones that performed poorly. So, we planned posts based on these ideas, and they performed better than ever.

By developing our standards of performance based on data, rather than gut feelings, we consistently created high-performing content. This happened because we did the analysis and disciplined ourselves to stick to the standards. We decided we shouldn't publish something unless it was the best content in its category on the whole damn internet.

How to Create the Best Content on Any Topic on the Internet

HOW TO CREATE THE BEST CONTENT ON ANY TOPIC ON THE INTERNET

- ☐ FIND THE KEYWORDS
- ☐ READ TOP 10 PAGES THAT RANK
- ☐ NOTE COMMONALITIES
- ☐ NOTE WHAT THEY'RE MISSING
- ☐ DRAFT COMPREHENSIVE OUTLINE

Figure 15.

Find the Keywords

Every piece of content we create is driven by strategic keyword research. This is because we want to optimize our content so our audience can find each piece when they need it most. However, our team goes further down the rabbit hole of Search Engine Optimization (SEO). We begin with a content core topic, then use tools like Moz (http://moz.com) and Ahrefs (http://ahrefs.com) to find a primary keyword or longtail phrase for it. We then outline three to five semantically related terms, which are simply terms closely related to your main keyword for which your content can also rank. Think of them as secondary keywords or phrases people may also search for when looking for content like the piece you're publishing.

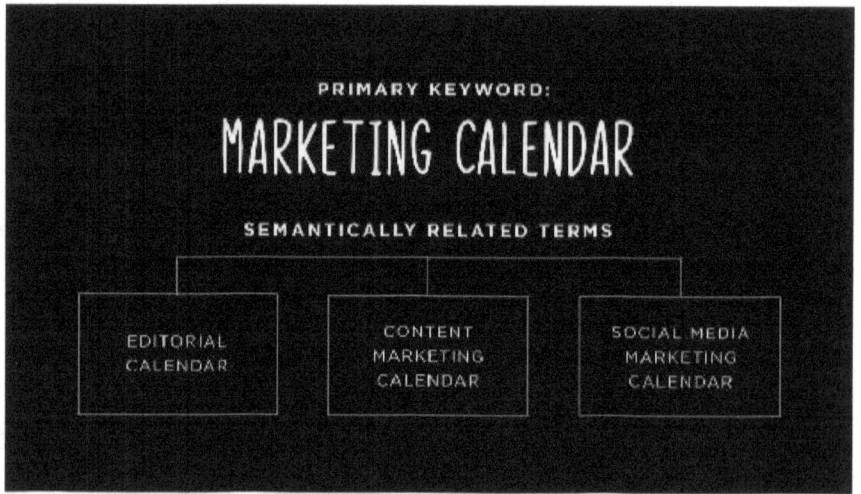

Figure 16.

You can find related terms with the keyword research tools I listed above. There is also an ever-evolving host of other tools to do the job.

The bottom line is that your content can rank for way more than one keyword or phrase. And that's where semantically related terms come in. They amplify your content in search results for the long haul.

Read Top 10 Pages That Rank

Next, we search Google using our exact primary keyword. Then, we read, watch, or listen to every single piece ranking on page one. This means we study the top ten performing pieces.

Note Commonalities

As we study these pieces, we note the commonalities they share. This means we look at things like:

Content length

Content structure

Custom graphics and visuals

Social media engagement by platform

Content upgrades

Actionability and comprehensiveness

Tone of voice

Number of comments

Unique angles covered

Point of view and controversy

Data and research used

Note What They're Missing

This careful survey then allows us to note what the top-ranking pieces are missing. This is a vital step so we can create competition-free content. We don't want to waste time talking about the same angles in the same ways as everyone else. That's a red ocean; we want to swim in the blue ocean. With this step, here are a handful of things we can define:

Seek out a unique angle no one has talked about.

This is a perfect place to not only find competition-free content but also to assert a contrary perspective. Controversy is attractive and interesting. So, if we disagree with someone, we'll say so, and then prove precisely why our experience and data support our point of view.

Find ways to be more actionable.

This often means going beyond tips and into the territory of showing people exactly how to do what we're talking about. When you do similar research, you'll often find thin content that tells people what to do, but not how to do it. This is a fantastic way to set your content apart.

Identify gaps in visuals and graphics.

With even a quick pass, you can see how graphically intense your competition is. Are they just using the low-hanging fruit of a stock photo as a header graphic? Or have they invested in custom design, infographics, videos, GIFs, or other visual content? This helps our content creators and designers determine how to go beyond the top-ranking pieces.

Draft a comprehensive outline.

Last, we take all of the research we've gathered and focus it into a comprehensive outline. This outline defines five things:

The opening hook, along with two or three complementary CoSchedule pieces we're going to link to.

The content upgrade that will increase value, add actionability, and therefore be worthy of an email or trial signup.

The body content, with subheads, includes the main keyword and related terms, as well as custom images to be designed.

The supporting data and research we will use to prove our assertions.

The next step, or action, we will call our audience to take.

In all, this process ensures we create the best damn content on the internet every single time. It takes work—but it's worth it. Here's the deal. If it feels easy, it's not competition-free content. Why? Because it's been done before. These five pillars of content creation ensure we nail our content core and create competition-free content.

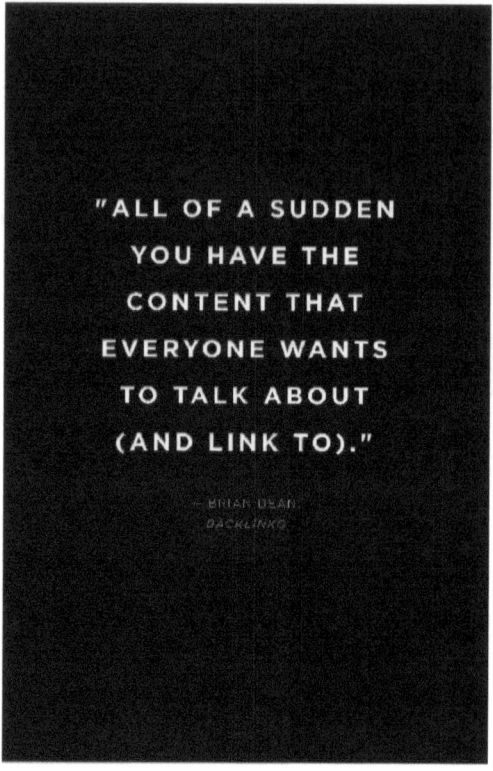

Figure 17.

10x Marketing Interview: Brian Dean and the Skyscraper Technique

As you can see, research plays a huge role in our content process. In fact, it's crucial to shipping 10x content every single week. But, you probably still have some questions. For instance, where should your ideas come from? If you've never had content produce big results for you, how do you figure out what has the greatest likelihood of short-circuiting the growth loop?

Whether you've experienced content marketing success or not, here's a simple, three-step hack that will work. It works so well, in fact, it's part of our own workflow. It's called the "Skyscraper Technique," and was developed by [Brian Dean of Backlinko](). Brian is a noted SEO authority and has used the technique to increase more than double his website traffic in less than two weeks after first putting it together.

Let's look at each step to put it to work in your 10x content.

Step One: Keyword Research

In Step One, you're really doing search engine optimization (SEO) work. You're finding the content core, competition-free topics you want to own in search. And even though the SEO landscape shifts continuously, the Skyscraper Technique focuses on this changeless factor: search will always begin with a keyword. Whether it's someone typing a phrase into a browser or using a voice search on their phone, this will necessarily hold true.

The goal of SEO research is obviously to find keywords your target customer is searching for. Overall, as Brian explains, keyword research that uncovers the intent behind people's searches is 75 percent of the game. To begin, brainstorm topics your target customer would search for when looking for information. Your keywords, or phrases, will fall into one of two categories: commercial keywords and informational keywords.

Commercial Keywords

Commercial keywords are the things your potential customers are searching for with credit card in hand. They're looking for a solution, and it's time to buy. For your company, these keywords will be closely tied to whatever you sell. However, they are often limited and highly competitive.

Informational Keywords

Second, there is a broader set of keywords called informational keywords. Researching these keywords is more nuanced. You must ask, "What are my customers searching for when they're not shopping for my product or service?" Then, list out all of the different topics they are searching for.

You can do this through customer conversations or even research on sites like Quora and Reddit. These keywords should be related to what you sell, but they don't have to be exact. For instance, if you were selling weight loss plans, your customer base is likely looking for things like workout routines and exercise equipment, as well. A perfect way to think about these things is as content core topics.

There are plenty of keyword research tools available to you, as well. There are too many to list or name here. But remember, if you can put a tool to work for you to save time and get better results, do it. A little research into the right SEO tools for you can go a long way.

Step Two: Analyze What's Ranking Now

After your research, it's time to analyze your competition. Simply read, watch, or consume every single piece of content that's currently ranking on the first page of Google for your chosen keyword. One of the mistakes Brian said he made early on was assuming if he created enough content, someday he would get more traffic from Google than everyone else—sort of like whoever has the biggest pile of content wins the game. However, he quickly realized that the path was futile. After all, every piece of content competes with hundreds of articles — including the ten top dogs on page one. It's a red ocean out there! So, if you create something that's even the tenth best on the internet, you're still not going to appear on page one of Google! It's not a volume game; it's a value game.

Step Three: 10x the Competition in the Face

Last, it's time to create content that's ten times better than the landscape you've just surveyed. One of the first articles Brian created using the Skyscraper Technique was about the roughly 200 ranking factors Google's algorithm used to rank web pages at the time. He knew the keyword phrase "Google ranking algorithm" was one he needed to own to become a leader in the SEO field.

So, he analyzed and read every top-ranking article for the keyword. And what he realized was that none of the articles had all of the ranking factors in one place. They may have had 50 percent of them—but not all. It was time to create his own piece of 10x content that added 20 levels plus a penthouse suite on top of the content skyscraper.

Brian created his content to be a one-stop shop for the topic. He made it as comprehensive as possible by curating every single published ranking factor. His resulting article provides an incredible experience for visitors. Because now, instead of having to track down the factors and cobble them all together themselves, they had it all right there in Brian's article.

There are endless ways to create content that's 10x better than the others. In this case, it was sheer comprehensiveness. Brian relates that he's also had success in 10x-ing design with detailed graphics, data-rich charts, infographics, companion videos, and real-life case studies.

This is a great opportunity to put a content scorecard to work, because, as Brian noted, "A common misstep is to overrate your own content, and underrate what's already on the first page." In the same way parents generally think their kids are the smartest and prettiest, our own content appears leagues better if we wear rose-colored glasses rather than look reality in the face.

Additionally, even if your content is better, it's truly a matter of degrees. Think about your content like a product. If you launch a new and improved product, but it's only 5 percent better than current solutions, it won't be enough to galvanize people into switching teams and buying from you. Your content is the same way. You must create something that is 10 times better—the 10x principle at work. You must blow the existing content out of the water with comprehensiveness, actionability, design, and value.

The Anatomy of 10x Content

The reason we're putting such an emphasis on how to create 10x content is that everything you create has a job to do. It must have utility for your company and your audience. Over the years, we've had a variety of ultra-successful content pieces. We've also published a bunch of duds. To bring creating 10x content in for a landing, I'll drill further into our content standards of performance.

Topic

The topic is always aligned with our content core. It needs to be well chosen to help both our intended audience and our company. This means it directly intersects with the value our product adds and with our audience's needs. No parallel topics allowed.

Research

Data, examples, and experience fuel 10x content. And each helps us make sure the angle we target is backed up with facts while proving our advice will produce big results after practical application. One of our most successful articles ever is entitled "What 20 Studies Say About The Best Times To Post On Social Media." It clocks in at roughly 5,500 words, contains dozens of custom images and infographics, and goes uber deep into the science behind social media posting. And just like the title suggests, it presents findings from twenty different studies to prove what we're talking about.

Actionability

In our content, we never simply sprinkle a few bites of free advice people will struggle to put to work for them. Instead, we publish work that includes research-fueled advice coupled with actionable, step-by-step guidance, deep attention to detail, and a path to execution. The audience should be able to do exactly what we're talking about if they follow the process we provide.

Content upgrade

Closely related to Actionability is our use of content upgrades. They help people put our teaching to work. But they also exist to attract potential customers to use CoSchedule as their marketing calendar. So, we optimize everything to convert traffic into email subscribers who will continue to get this awesome, actionable content from us while also giving us the opportunity to share more information about the tool we offer that helps organize the chaos of content marketing.

Single CTA

To the end of content serving a business use, everything we do includes a single, clear call to action. We aren't trying to get our audience to do three or four different things on a page. We want them to do one thing, and we make that one action abundantly clear. Whether it's to sign up for our email list or trial our product, every piece of content has a clear next step for our audience to take.

We'll devote an entire chapter to CTAs and conversion psychology. But it's important to mention this here because revenue-generating action is the purpose of 10x content.

Graphics

Design has been a mainstay of our making our content competition-free from the beginning. We invest heavily in custom graphics in all our content, from blog posts to podcasts to webinars. As an example, we design between five and seven custom graphics for each piece. And, we design custom images for every social network, as well. High-caliber design immediately sets your content apart while also providing an opportunity to be useful to your audience. Visuals help reinforce and illustrate key concepts in our content.

Structure

The web is different from printed media. Blogs aren't books, and microsites aren't magazines, so, you need to write differently for the web compared to other media. Our content uses a structure that employs frequent visual breaks:

We use short paragraphs that are rarely more than three sentences long.

We use callouts for quotes and takeaway statements.

We use lots of bulleted and numbered lists.

Content Marketing

We use the Click-to-Tweet plugin so our audience can share impact statements with a simple click or tap.

And finally, we organize our content well with subheads to guide the reader through the content.

Structure, though seemingly simplistic, is a vital part of the user experience. This is especially true for people reading our content on mobile devices. These best practices ensure a seamless experience on any screen.

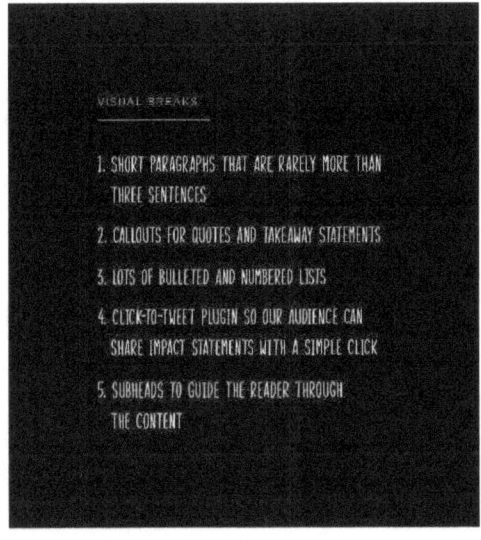

Figure 19.

How to Use a Content Scorecard

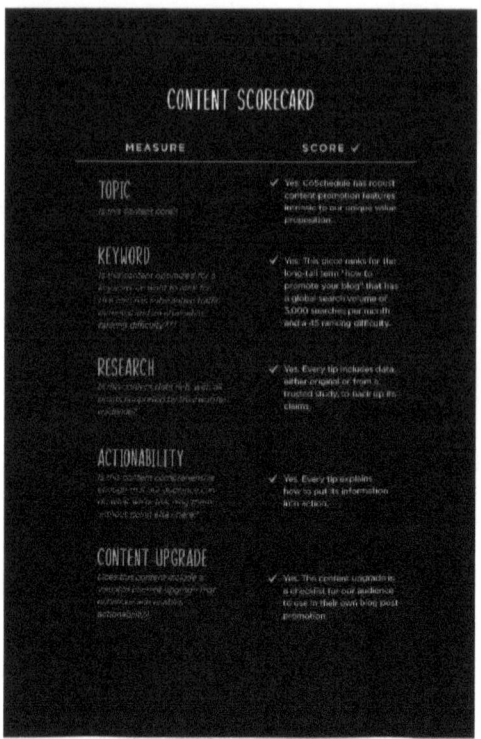

Figure 20.

* According to Ahrefs: "Traffic potential shows how much organic search traffic you can possibly get if you rank #1 for the Parent Topic keyword. We estimate this traffic potential by looking at the organic search traffic of the current #1 ranking result for that Parent topic keyword."

Content Marketing

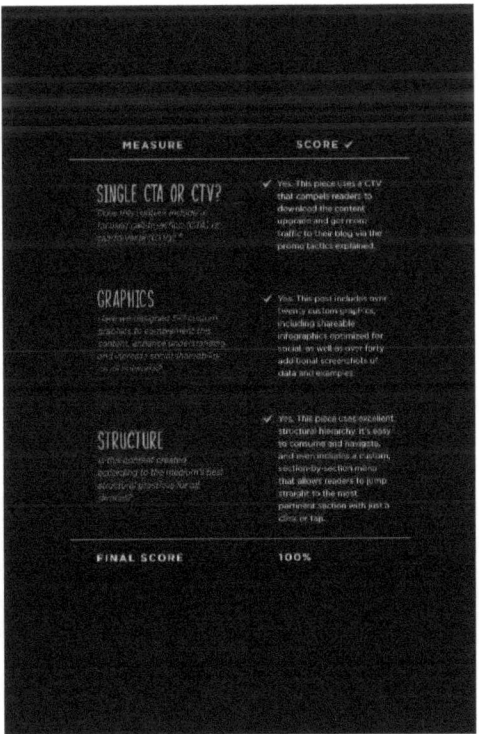

Figure 21.

* We will discuss CTAs and CTVs at length in Chapter 13, "Conversion Psychology." But for context, a CTA compels your audience to take immediate action, such as, "Sign Up Free Now—No Credit Card Required." A CTV compels your audience to enter the next stage of your marketing funnel by inviting them to value, such as, "Get More Traffic To Your Blog Posts Within 7 Days."

This blog post met every benchmark of our content scorecard. So, how did it perform? In its first thirty days alone, it generated 23,358 page views and 21 trial signups. In the following six months, it scored nearly 150,000 pageviews and is ranked solidly in the number one position on Google for its keyword. In fact, it's even captured the coveted "Featured Snippet," which Google explains this way:

How To Promote Your Blog With Social Media

1. Share your content in many places. ...
2. Include your blog link in your social media profiles.
 ...
3. Rock the power of 100 rule. ...
4. Clean up your open graph data. ...
5. Share your blog posts on social media right when you publish them. ...
6. Share your brand new posts more than once.

More items...

How To Promote Your Blog With 107 Content Promotion Tactics
https://coschedule.com/blog/how-to-promote-your-blog/

Figure 22.

Google search for the term "how to promote your blog."

Creating Your Own Content Scorecard

Both Jeff Goins's content scorecard and ours at CoSchedule have proven invaluable. By holding your content to a high standard, you can also identify likely performance gaps before you publish. So, what about your content? Do you have a content scorecard that drives what you publish?

If not, now's the time to create one. Or heck, you can even swipe Jeff's or ours! Remember, statistically, your content is the functional homepage for your website. So, if your site is going to produce real business results, your content needs to meet the standards of performance to which you'd hold any other marketing effort. To create your own scorecard, start simply, and use this basic framework of questions:

What is our content's goal?

What characteristics are present in the content we've published that has accomplished this goal?

Is the topic within our content core?

Creating a content scorecard isn't enough, though. It also requires discipline to stick to it. Saying, "No, we won't publish this piece until it meets our criteria," is a big step. But you, and your team must commit yourselves to the practice if it's going to work. As with every part of the 10x Marketing Formula, the magic happens when you put it into practice. It's on you to make it happen. But when you do, you'll see results.

This Is Your Shot

This chapter could be summarized like this: create every piece of content with the assumption that it's your only shot at publishing the best piece of content ever produced on that topic. This will mandate well-researched 10x content that performs in line with your scorecard. It means creating stuff that wows your audience to capitalize on the halo effect, thus bestowing love on every new page visited, and even your product itself.

Every piece of content you create is your one shot to get results on your website. So, the primary question to ask when you start, and right before you publish, is this: "Will this content turn readers into customers by taking the next step in the process?"

Action is the measure of success—and creating a content scorecard is the place to begin.

Your 10x Toolbox

Put this chapter into action with your 10x Toolbox by visiting https://coschedule.com/10x-toolbox

10x Marketing Interview: Jeff Goins and the Content Scorecard

In this interview, author and speaker Jeff Goins explains how his team developed the content scorecard—a tool he says transformed their results. You will have access to the full audio interview plus transcript.

[Template] 10x Content Scorecard

This template helps you score your content before it's ever published. It's a dead simple way for ensuring consistent quality and measuring potential impact before a piece is published.

10x Marketing Interview:

Brian Dean and the Skyscraper Technique

[Checklist] The Skyscraper Technique Checklist

This is a checklist for using Brian's "Skyscraper Technique" for content research and creation.

[Free Tool] Headline Analyzer

The Headline Analyzer is a free tool that will help you write headlines that drive traffic, shares, and search results. It is available absolutely free at: https://coschedule.com/headline-analyzer

A Short message from the Author:

Hey, are you enjoying the book? I'd love to hear your thoughts!

Many readers do not know how hard reviews are to come by, and how much they help an author.

I would be incredibly grateful if you could take just 60 seconds to write a brief review on Amazon, even if it's just a few sentences!

\>> Click here to leave a quick review

https://www.amazon.com/review/create-review?asin=XXXXXXXXX

Thank you for taking the time to share your thoughts!

Your review will genuinely make a difference for me and help gain exposure for my work.

Chapter 4
Who are you writing for?

"All progress takes place outside the comfort zone."

– Michael John Bobak

Imagine you're opening a restaurant.

You've found a nice place in the center of your home town next to a popular bar.

What do you do next? Design a trendy interior? Look for local suppliers? Go chat with the bar owner next door to do a co-promotion?

Let's say you start with creating your menu. How many starters do you need? How many main courses? And how many main courses should be vegetarian?

You start wondering—who will come to your restaurant? Will they prefer to eat meat, or fish, or vegetarian fare? And do they like a traditional menu or more adventurous dishes? Should the food be spicy or not?

Just like with a restaurant, you need to know who your blog readers are before you start writing. Readers have a choice of millions of blogs. Why will they choose to spend their precious time reading your blog posts?

If you don't know who you're writing for, your blog may go in myriad directions, and you end up speaking to no one. So how can you ensure your blog posts speak strongly to your target audience?

In this chapter, you learn:

- Why you should write your blog for one ideal reader only
- What to do if your blog targets more than one audience
- How to create your ideal reader profile

Why is the Strategy Behind Free Content So Important?

The problem isn't the Internet. It was the kind of subscribers they were attracting. Also, they were sending out the wrong kind of content. You can't just create content full of tips or even step-by-step guidance. There has to be something more. You have to make a personal connection with your audience. That means integrating with your own stories or even case studies from other clients. Think about a professional speaker or an author you admire. You've probably gained a lot of value from them, but I bet you it's not the step-by-step systems you remember most. It's the stories they tell. Every professional speaker knows the audience will forget their five tips before they even walk off the stage, but they remember the stories for years to come.

Your Strategic Myth includes your origin story, but it goes beyond this. It's a story about a dream. It's about overcoming challenges. It's about a hero who wouldn't take NO for an answer. There is a story inside you that you have to share with the world. And you're inviting them in along on your journey. You're inviting them to take part in your story and your mission.

There is already too much content online. You're not going to cut through all the noise online by publishing just another series of boring articles. You have to grab your prospects by the lapels and give them a story that will stick with them. It has to be memorable. It has to be entertaining. And it has to be something they want to share with others. What story are you telling? Is it a story about just another business that wants a share of their hard-earned cash? Or is it an exciting story that inspires them?

By the end of this book, you will know who your ideal clients are. You will have a story to tell that they identify with. And you will know how to get your message out there using simple step-by-step methods that are proven to work in virtually every market.

Chapter 5
The Profile of a Copywriter

"The only limit to our realization of tomorrow will be our doubts of today."

– Franklin D. Roosevelt

If you have read so far, you may wonder (as I would do) why should you become a copywriter? How would you know you are fit for this kind of job?

Let me give you two reasons that convinced me a while ago:

- Even if it is one of the most competitive writing fields in the industry, is also one of the most lucrative;

- You find out if you have what it takes to be a great copywriter going through the following list. It is not necessarily a rule. The list puts together a personal point of view, but you will see that most of the professionals recommend the same.

Therefore, for successful content marketing you need:

To have a little bit of talent

I say a little bit because talent values too little if it is not accompanied by constant hard work. Talent in writing is not something that you have since you are a child. You discover it in time, and only after you have tried some samples. This part gets me to the second skill:

You love to write

I always believed that I was no good at writing, but I've loved writing since I've known myself. Therefore, if you love writing you most likely have a seed of talent in you. You will find some people that have talent and do not like to write, but this comes, from my point of view, as a natural hazard of the job.

Of course, you may have periods when you will be bored of writing, but this does not mean you cannot become a copywriter. I believe everybody experiences boredom from time to time. When you find yourself in such a period, take a short break, remember the reasons that drove you to (copy)writing and rediscover the passion in you.

I like to think that content marketing is like being in a long-term relationship with words. I do not give up; I just take it one step at a time and tackle difficult periods in a calm and relaxing manner. Talent, passion, and a lot of hard work will lead you to great jobs (and great amounts of money).

Be willing to start at low prices

I want you to understand that your job is worth the money, it's just that you need to be realistic! When you start as a beginner, you need to build up your portfolio to create a network. Until you get there, you should enter the market by having lower prices. I will tell you about how to charge for your work later on.

Be confident about being different

A copywriter can write for all sorts of businesses and in different areas. To become successful, you need to become an expert in only one field. Having a specialty increases credibility. Or, in other words, do not become a general writer. You discover the right niche for you by trying. Write copies for different niches. The ones that are easiest to do should be in the field that you will most likely become an expert in.

Be prepared to sell yourself

This part was the hardest for me. However, some sales skills will ease your way into earning 6 figures. Research how other people market themselves and find your own way. You can start a blog, in which you upload your portfolio (or samples), make your marketing strategy, and create a product around your services. At this point, do not be afraid of people who criticize you. Take their comments as feedback, and improve.

Be prepared to become a Nazi grammar

Be able to observe punctuation and grammar. Even if many people know a lot about writing and even love to do it, their content has grammar or punctuation errors. In content marketing, such errors are unacceptable. No problem at this point. However, you need to improve in this regard (if necessary) and double check the writing every time. The content is equally important to punctuation and proper grammar.

Develop Patience

In any new career, the beginning requires time and a lot of hard work. You will also deal with different clients, some more pleasant than others. Hence, you will need a lot of patience to deal with so-called "problematic" clients (I will detail below a short typology of "difficult" clients and how to deal with them).

A desire to speak up, with objectivity and humility

I put in here three qualities, that one needs to meet to be a successful copywriter. The part about speaking up is a must, as copywriters also express opinion/point of view. This is a harder aspect for shy individuals, but they can get away with it with practice (start speaking up in a group of close friends and with family).

The areas of objectivity and humility go hand in hand. The facts from your copy need to be analyzed as objectively as possible, so you offer the customer the closest point of view to reality. On top of this, no one likes misleading information.

As for humility, this will help you acknowledge your limits, and do your best with everything you know. Accept and use feedback. Never assume that you are too good. Even the best copywriters have things to improve on

Strategy and creativity

The easiest way to explain this: as your job as a copywriter requires you to address a specific audience; you need to create your content in such a way that you impress that audience. The two essential tools for this are: well-targeted strategy and a lot of creativity. Also, keep in mind that one does not go without the other.

Be available to write samples

In the beginning, when you do not have a portfolio yet, you will need to write samples to convince potential customers of your skills. Of course, you can use the best examples that you have already written in your "training" period. Keep in mind at this point (and every time you write something) to be original. Plagiarism is a definite no.

Content Marketing

Be open to new opportunities

Having such a lucrative job, you may find new opportunities in places and within businesses you would have never expected. You will not be a beginner for the rest of your life, so, as you gain experience and your network expands, continue to search for better and more appealing projects.

Having all these, a copywriter will be able to:

Write/change a piece of content into a functional one;

I talk about functionality because the purpose of content marketing is, after all, to make content functional, to promote something, or to highlight an opinion. It has to have a high impact on readers. In a nutshell, a copywriter uses the skills of a writer and techniques of a copywriter to say something that captures audience attention.

Sell a product/service

This is the main functionality of content marketing content. Once the customer's attention is on the product, the words need to convince them to try that product. Hence, the piece of writing has to be both appealing and informative. The best copywriters (already) have the skills to focus solely on the main points that will determine whether the customer will buy the product/service.

Persuade the consumer

The end of each copy should contain what is called a "call to action". Therefore, after reading, each customer will (or not) be convinced to try, buy or promote the product/service advocated in the article/piece of writing. This requires from the copywriter, a high level of understanding of the readers and the target audience.

Use different styles of writing

Although many copywriters have a distinct way of writing, professional copywriters have the skills and ability to use different styles. The point is to be able to adapt the content to the target market language. For example, the language is different for children, adults working in big companies, or older people.

Create Solutions

A good ad is one that can answer a customer's problems. Customers look for products or services because they need that particular product or service in their lives. As a copywriter, it's your job to let these people know about how these certain products/services can make their lives easier and better.

Here are two things that you have to keep in mind:

- Define what the problem is. The "problem" refers to something that's missing in the customers' lives. For example, some may have the need for a brand-new perfume, cheap alternative medicine, the best dating website, or affordable flowers for a wedding among other things. Basically, every person out there has something that they need in their life. Target these needs and come up with a solution for it.

- Explain what you have to offer in a unique, catchy way. Lure the customers to you in such a way that other advertisers haven't done before. Be unique in creating solutions or copy. This is the only way you'll know if your copy can help your clients get the kind of profit that they want and if their services/products become popular, or at least, better known than they already are.

That's basically what you have to remember. Define the problem, come up with a solution, and voila! You'll be able to create a great copy.

Here are some examples of great copies that you can pattern your ads from:

Let's say your client asks you to create a public advisory as part of an anti-smoking campaign. Here's something that you can do:

"Want to learn more about lung cancer? Keep smoking."

This example is simple but very effective because it will hit people's minds in a way where they will easily make a connection between lung cancer and smoking. Thus, they will think that the more they smoke, the higher their chances of getting lung cancer are. It's as simple as that.

Next, if there's a product in the market that is gaining popularity, but the client wants it to be better known by more people or wants people to gain greater awareness about it, here's what you can do:

Let's say the product is a perfume.

"Haven't tried Fantasy by Britney Spears? Then you're surely missing out on something. It's great. It's powerful. It's fantasy."

Let people know that they are missing out on something because this will surely catch their attention. When people realize that they haven't tried something that others have already tried, then they will feel like they are not in the know, and thus, they will want to try that certain something right away. See? It's easy and effective.

You can also take a hint from classic Zippo ads. Zippos are lighters that are popular for their classic and stylish look as well as their longevity in the industry. One of the old Zippo ads bear the lines "Don't lose your Zippo. Lifetime friends are rare." This means that Zippos are a great investment because they can last for a really long time and they are truly reliable. Creating ads like this will surely boost your profits and your clients' profits as well.

Another tip would be to learn how to make sure that your text or copy on the image is used in the advertisement. There's a Duracell advertisement wherein a girl plays with a doll, and another older doll comes inside the house. The lines "Some toys last forever" are written next to the old doll. This refers to the fact that Duracell batteries are sturdy, reliable, and can last for a long time, which means that it would be good for anyone to buy them.

Humor is also very important. There's an ad for the restaurant 321 East that goes something like this: "How good is our steak? Last week, a man was choking on a piece and refused the Heimlich maneuver." Morbid as it may sound, this shows that someone was willing to die for a product that this restaurant is offering! Well, of course, this incident isn't true, but it can get people's attention and makes people curious as to how the steak tastes like. This is a very effective kind of copy.

Another great ad would be a one from Play-Doh. Beside the image of a can of Play-Doh, the line "Included: A lightsaber, a dinosaur, a rocket, transforming cars, toy soldiers, a spaceship, etc." are written. As you may well know by now, Play-Doh is a kind of clay modeling compound that's used to create different kinds of shapes and objects beyond your imagination. When kids see this, they will be more likely to bug their parents to buy them the said product, and thus, it proves to be an effective way of advertising.

Style Formatting

Make Your Content Visually Attractive

There are subtle aspects of content you must pay attention to:

The font

You must post your content in a font that is large enough and easy to read. As mentioned earlier, the internet has bred a generation of skimming readers with increasingly shorter attention spans. Clarity and visual communication such as attractive images help you retain them for longer on your site or copy.

Use short paragraphs

Internet content requires information that is carefully delivered in short paragraphs with each paragraph addressing a specific salient subject. Cramming too much information in a single paragraph does not help your writing in this generation of skimming and short attention spans.

Word Play

Writers have a natural tendency to want to play with words. Overplaying with words is fine when writing for writing's sake or for other literary goals. However, content marketing is about selling. If you are an English major and you happen to be reading this, you need to take a careful audit of the direction your writing is headed. Content marketing is salesmanship, not about wordsmithing. Content marketing needs you to arrest the reader's interest at the slightest opportunity.

Consequently, flowery styles such as those English majors learn in school will only usher your prospect out of the site without converting. This is the reason why choosing action verbs over flowery adjectives does it for content marketing. In fact, an efficient copywriter does not care too much about grammar if breaking it will deliver best. There is an interesting quip by one Gary Bencivenga, a proliferate blogger and writer, that a copywriter who shows off their writing prowess by playing with words is like a fisherman who shows off their hook.

Break the Rules

Observing convention is great. However, as a sales writer, you need to rediscover what makes a prospect tick. It is said that while on their colonization expeditions, imperialists in many places used religious approaches to get to their subjects. They appealed to the sense of security that religion offered. They appealed to what people needed. Religious values were palatable to the subjects; therefore, the imperialists ceased the chance to get their subjects to listen. The hidden agenda of expanding empires came much later after striking a chord with the locals.

Acceptability

Similarly, a good copywriter must understand the language of the customer, i.e. the readership. You must attune your writing to the needs of the prospect you have in mind. Consequently, you must use the names they use for what they want. This is the only way you are going to convince them that you don't preach water and drink wine. They will see you as one of them; that you understand them and that you know what they really need. The point here is to get the reader to feel you. Think in their language to you grasp their perspective. Only then will you identify a clear meeting point. Grammar nuance isn't going to persuade your prospect but the touch and persuasion coupled of course with the actual value they perceive you add to their lives.

Chapter 6
Clients Want Proven Results

"The harder the conflict, the more glorious the triumph."

– Thomas Paine

When it comes to content marketing, clients want proven results. They don't want to hire someone who may have simply written a few articles in the past and then hopefully will be able to put together a whole campaign to sell a product. They want someone who has experience, someone who has done this work before, can prove that the work was successful, and show that these clients are willing to pay a premium to get this.

Most clients understand that they are going to get what they pay for. If they are going to spend money on this campaign, and they want to make money on their product, they understand that they need to pick out a copywriter who knows what they are doing and can bring in results. The client would rather pay a little bit more to get the good results the first time rather than paying someone new to do the work, wasting time and money, and then having to pay the professional to come in and clean up the mess.

You will find that good clients know how much you are worth. If you are working with a client that wants to pay a low rate, there are a few things that are going on here. First, the client is either not aware of the current rate for a good copywriter and is just guessing at how much they will need to pay for the work to get done. Another issue could be that they are having issues with their cash flow and they are hoping for a miracle to happen, such as a good content marketing offering to do the services for a great price so they can get their business back up and running. And in other cases, the client is just trying to get work for free - they don't really care how hard you work, as long as they get the results that they want for a way below market value amount.

No matter the reason for the lower amount offered on a job, you don't want to work with any of these clients. The first client doesn't know your true value and may be difficult to work within the long term. Now you can talk to them about the price and some will realize that they need to pay more and will be happy to do it, but others will still want to get the discounted price because that is all they want to pay and they think the work is "easy enough for anyone to do." You don't want to work for these people because they won't value your work and you will spend way too much time making very little money.

For the second group of clients, you need to be careful. There is usually a reason that they are short on cash or have cash flow issues, and often this means that they are about to fail. You are not only going to miss out on some of the good income that you should be making, but the company is likely going to fail and you won't make a good income at all from them.

And finally, no one wants to work with someone who purposely puts the value too low. Many times, these clients disappear and never even pay, leaving you with a lot of wasted time and no money to show for it. Even if the client does end up paying you for the work that you do, you will find that they are really difficult to work with, will request way too many changes, and you will spend more time than it is worth to get the work done.

Finding the clients who will pay the rates that you deserve is critical. This is going to help out in a number of ways. First, they are going to value your time. Perhaps these clients have worked with some bad copywriters in the past and they are willing to pay more to get the results that they want, or they know the market value for what they want. Once you prove that you are the person they want to work with, you are going to be able to get those well-paying jobs that are going to make your income go through the roof.

But before you can work for these better prices, you need to make sure that you are able to produce those results. There are plenty of clients that will pay attractive rates but are not going to pay those rates to just anyone. You will need to have a method to show how you have been successful with these kinds of campaigns in the past. You will need to show some of the work that you have done with content marketing in the past, and if you have some numbers in place to show how successful they were, you will be able to impress the clients even more.

As a good copywriter, you should be able to show that you are going to bring in results for the client. A good client is willing to pay some of the higher rates, but you do need to make it worth their time. These clients are going to pay for the results, not just for your time to create the work. If there aren't any results, you are going to have some issues getting the income that you want.

The Power of Landing Pages

In the digital marketing and online business community, landing pages are crucial. They're the difference between a successful campaign and one that makes you question the results people claim to be getting.

The wrong ones will make the internet spew hate and vitriol then push you into a downward spiral leading to a long, slow, agonizing death.

The right landing pages turn browsers to fans, haters to friends, and customers to advocates. People share them on social media and the world creates hashtags in your honor.

There's a fine line between high performing landing pages and the ones that'll make you wonder if the time you spent on them was worth it.

Old advice like "use red in your headlines" and "create multiple columns on your pages" will kill conversions faster than a prize-winning thanksgiving turkey gets slaughtered.

Your audience is jaded.

They've been on the web for years. Many of them were born into the web and may know more about it than you.

You're doing yourself, your brand, and your customers a disservice by trying to get away with poorly designed and researched landing pages.

Why?

Because I know how powerful they are when used correctly. It's even more pronounced when you don't have much traffic. If your website is receiving a million visitors a month, you can disregard this book because you'll get customers and subscribers no matter what you do.

If you're like the rest of us mortals, then keep reading. You'll find gems in this book and learn how to create more powerful landing pages that move your business forward.

Before we dive into making the ultimate landing pages, you and I need to be on the same page.

A visitor can "land" on any page.

While those pages can and should be optimized for conversions (especially the about page, as it is one of the top three visited pages on a website), they're not what I'm referring to when I say landing page.

Whenever you see "landing pages" in this book, it refers to dedicated pages made and optimized to do one thing:

That could be to make a sale.

That could be to promote a sign up for a mailing list.

It could also be to promote a giveaway.

Whatever.

The overarching theme with the landing pages I discuss is they have one desired outcome. The rest of the pages on your website have too many distractions. Those include links in the body text, menu buttons, popups, footer links, a sidebar, etc.

Let's redefine landing pages to reflect the focus of this book.

Content Marketing

Landing pages are standalone web pages distinct from your main website that has been designed for a single focused objective. This means your landing page shouldn't have global navigation, in-text links, or extraneous elements like a sidebar.

There are many types of landing pages.

1. Click through pages. These are pages, generally on e-commerce websites, used to promote clicking through to the next page where the sale can be made. Think of them as teaser pages which warm up the prospect for the main offer.

2. Lead generating pages. This is the most common type of landing page. Their focus is to get your visitor to part with their contact information so you can market to them later in a more controlled setting EG Email.

It's done by giving away something of value in exchange for the contact information. A few examples of lead magnets are:

- E-books
- Webinars
- Cheat sheets
- Video tutorials
- First chapter of a book
- Free consultations
- Contests

- Free trial

- Notifications on updates

- Whitepaper

3. Sales pages. The most important pages on your website. This is where the money is made and, by nature, has the lowest conversion rate. On average, e-commerce sites see a 2%-4% conversion rate, and SaaS companies see 3%-5% conversions.

Of course, your product or service could be a necessity, novelty, or other –ty that makes it convert much higher.

What kind of assumptions, you ask?

Well, for starters, you assume your headline is good. You assume your button placement is the best. You assume your offer resonates with your customers. You assume your copy is well written. You assume these and dozens of other things.

Those assumptions should be tested at every turn by data. You observe and react to the data. It doesn't matter what your gut says if the data doesn't back it up.

At times, the process can be tedious and discouraging. I want to let you know the tangible benefits you'll receive as a result of an optimized landing page. Look back at this list when you get tired of the optimization process and want to throw in the towel.

It'll always be worth it.

Benefits of Landing Pages

I'm only going to touch on a few of the many benefits of landing pages. There are so many, I could write a book solely on this.

I digress.

The versatility of landing pages is what makes them so powerful. You can change colors, fonts, images, copy, and anything else you want with just a few keystrokes and button clicks.

Try doing that with the design you paid your developer for. Or what about the marketing videos you're thinking about making. How hard will those be to change?

Anyway, let's move into the most powerful positives of landing pages.

Skyrocket Website Conversions

What if you had a three-page website? One page is your homepage. The other page is your about page. The last page is a landing page optimized for sales. You may convert at a few percentage points. More likely, you'll convert at below a percentage point.

What happens when you have dozens of landing pages in addition to the three pages I just mentioned?

You have one for giving away an e-book, you have another one for a nice tool, another one gives away a piece of software. Oh, I forgot the one you have for a free consultation. Together, the dozens of landing pages bring more than 10x your subscriber conversion rate.

Every subscriber you gain is another opportunity for a sale. With email marketing, you'll blow your normal conversion rate out of the water.

This isn't a book on email marketing, but the two go hand in hand. The increased conversions via landing pages, coupled with a strong email marketing campaign will do wonders for your bottom line.

Data gathering and usage behavior

It's the internet. We're all connected. Whether that's good for us as individuals is up for debate. There's no denying its good news for your business.

Imagine you're getting poor conversions on your product pages. You drill down into the data and realize most of your visitors are using Chrome and Safari browsers. You also notice you're getting much better conversion rates from visitors using Firefox and Internet Explorer.

You could ignore it, but you dive deeper and realize the difference is statistically significant (that means it's not a fluke).

You use an Android device and Mozilla Firefox when you access your pages. You've not experienced any issues when browsing.

You forget about it and start doing something else. While you're working, you can't shake the feeling that something's wrong. You can't ignore what you saw, so you borrow your friends iPhone and navigate to your landing page.

The images aren't lining up well, the text is off center, and the page looks like it was dug up from the nineties.

You're stunned.

You download Google Chrome and navigate to the page. The same thing happens. Elements aren't where they're supposed to be, your font colors are off, and it looks like a child put the page together.

You're mortified.

How many people saw this page and decided your business sucked? After all, what kind of company can't even put a page together correctly?

You figured out an important piece of information with just one data point. Imagine what you can do when you have multiple data points to compare.

Sure, Google analytics gives you information, but dedicated landing page software gives you the data you need without having to prepare tedious custom reports. I've been there; it's not fun or easy.

This is a more extreme example, but when you have accurate data to work with, you'll begin to understand gaps and see patterns you can exploit.

Better Data Backed Decisions

With better data come better decisions. I talked about the ability to gather data at the last point. Now, I want to talk about what you can do with that data. In business, you need to know your costs and the effectiveness of your distribution channels, right?

If a direct mail piece is pulling $500 in profit for every one-hundred spent, you'll ramp it up – right?

The same applies to the web. If your Facebook ad campaign is pulling in profits then you'll put more money behind it.

Of course.

With the vast amount of data you'll be able to collect, like where people came from, which ones became customers, which traffic source bounced, how long they stayed on the page, etc. you'll make better decisions.

How would you change your campaigns if you realized the thousand dollars you spent on Facebook was only bringing in half as much as the thousand you spend on Instagram?

I bet you'd cut your Facebook ad spend and refocus it on Instagram.

Your decisions cease to be made based on how you feel. They become decisions you're confident in. It's no longer "we do it like this because it's always been done like this" to "we do it like this because we've run the tests."

You make better decisions when you have better data. Hold your data inviolate.

Build Hype and Validate Products/Ideas

How do you think people feel about your product or service? Unless it's a matter of life or death, it'll get old.

When Facebook appeared on the scene, it didn't have one-tenth of the bells and whistles it does now. It was a place to catch up with friends and follow companies you like. Now, there are ads everywhere, you keep getting requests to play games, and it tracks your movements in the real world.

It's a bit creepy.

Even though we criticize the way Facebook has changed, it wouldn't be here today if it would've stayed the same.

No matter what you're doing or selling, you need to create variety in your business.

If you've had only a few products, landing pages are a way to introduce new products gradually while testing market feedback.

If your blog is playful and laid back, landing pages are an outlet to get down to serious business. It's your choice how you introduce variety. Landing pages just happen to be an amazing vehicle for it.

Cater to more User Segments

This follows on the heels of variety. You may have one or only a few products and not need anymore. Even if that's the case, your customers will use your product differently.

Take Pinterest for example.

The main website was built for a certain demographic of people. Those are well to do, educated, and married women. In 2017, men have become the largest growing segment of their user base.

Those are for the users — the buyers. They have another section of their website entirely for advertisers and business owners. These people are the ones who are paying the bills and need resources and tools to make the most out of Pinterest.

It's not limited to marketplace type businesses or social media. Think about a photographer. They take pictures at weddings, birthdays, bar mitzvahs, and everything in between. When someone lands on their website, they want information relating to their specific situation. They don't want the generic spiel.

You can apply the same principle to almost any industry. The financial services sector needs different faces for students, young workers, high net worth individuals, and businesses.

The construction industry builds retail spaces, homes, and multi-unit housing complexes. Do you think those people need the same information? No, they don't. They need content, images, and offers related to their specific situation.

Even if you don't have dozens of products, you have different user segments which have different needs. The more optimized landing pages you have, the more opportunities there are to connect with different market segments.

Improve Marketing Campaigns

One of my biggest pet peeves is clicking on a link for a specific item and being dumped on the homepage. Yes, the homepage may have some of the information I'm looking for, but I have to keep clicking to get the entire story.

Why?

Why would you make me do extra work? Every extra step I have to take is an added layer of resistance. Unless I'm a highly motivated buyer, I'm likely to bounce and never return.

The good news is that most websites are waking up and sending individuals to specific landing pages: not all, but most.

Landing pages improve marketing campaigns because you're able to drill down into the needs of a specific group of people. It can be a campaign which deals with your new vacuum cleaner, but there are different types of people who need it.

You have the single mom, you have the college student, and you have the elderly couple.

For each of these groups, you'll highlight different benefits to the potential customer. For the single mom, it could be how affordable and durable it is. For the elderly couple, you can touch on how quiet and easy to use it is. You can lead with low maintenance and its chic design when talking to college students (and how cheap it is).

Every marketing campaign and segment within that campaign should have a dedicated landing page. I know that's not always possible for various reasons. Chief of which is data and time, but it's something to strive for when optimizing your pages.

Put List Building on Steroids

This is the most popular use of your landing pages. It's almost as important as using them for sales pages.

Almost.

The sidebar on your website works, but many people experience blindness. Think about how you personally use websites. Do you give the sidebar more than a passing glance?

No?

Neither does the rest of the world. Most websites don't make it worth your time. They add ugly graphics, uglier opt-in forms, and the occasional greatest hits collection. < what does this mean in context?

On average, the sidebar conversion rate hovers between 0.5% and 1%. Those are good numbers. Most websites don't achieve that without rigorous testing.

Dedicated landing pages are a different beast. On average, conversion rates climb well into the teens. For every 100 people that visit a landing page created to get contact details, 15-20 of them will become email subscribers.

I'm sure you know as well as I do that email subscribers are the bread and butter of cost-effective marketing campaigns.

With an optimized landing page, those numbers can easily double or triple. It's not by accident. A landing page focuses the attention and gives your prospect two options.

Either they perform your desired action or they exit the page. There aren't a bunch of miscellaneous links for them to click on, no menu buttons, and only one call to action.

Improve Credibility

Last but not least, landing pages improve your credibility in the eyes of your visitors.

Let me explain.

Throughout your website, you have elements scattered about. Maybe you have featured logos on the about page and homepage.

You also have testimonials on different portions of your website. They work together to let the people visiting know you're credible. In addition to that, you have a great design and other things going for you.

With a landing page, you incorporate those elements into one page.

You have testimonials, featured logos, and a unique design all on one page. You use persuasive language and pull out the big guns to establish trust.

Instead of someone needing to navigate to the homepage, then the about page, then the testimonials page, and maybe a few blog posts, you do the work for them with a well-designed landing page. It's a shortcut to the credibility needed to make a sale.

In a nutshell, landing pages are an asset. The more you have, the greater your conversions across the board. In a 2016 study, it was discovered that conversions went up by 55% once a website had ten or more landing pages.

That means just one landing page won't cut it. Five landing pages won't cut it either. It's a constant process of creation and iteration.

Throughout the rest of this book, you're going to be equipped with the insights and strategies to turn your landing pages into works of art.

Chapter 7
Content Marketing For Facebook Marketing

"A successful man is one who can lay a firm foundation with the bricks that others throw at him."

– David Brinkley

In the content marketing industry itself, there are niches that you can also specialize in. One particular content marketing niche where demand for experts is increasing is social media.

Facebook is the undisputed champion of all social networking websites. Many websites have risen from obscurity by using Facebook alone as a marketing tool. Websites that struggled to gain traction when using search engine marketing are turning to Facebook marketing as an alternative solution.

Facebook Content Marketing

Facebook is successful because of its ability to retain people's attention. The features on a user's profile page and timeline are so engaging that many people tend to spend hours on these pages without being aware of it. Companies and smaller businesses take advantage of these features by making sure that their posts show in these pages.

To be an excellent Facebook copywriter, you should first be familiar of the common objectives of companies and business that are using this social network as a marketing tool. Here are the common goals of companies that market on Facebook:

- Product/company introduction
- Awareness
- Popularity
- Event promotion
- Increase online and offline sales

Before you can start marketing on Facebook, you should first identify the need of your clients in their marketing campaign. If they are not aware of their marketing goals yet, then help them establish their goals by interviewing them and analyzing their motives.

Helping reach their goals through content marketing

When content marketing for Facebook, you have your own tasks to help the clients achieve their marketing goals. First, you need to get the user's attention. Then, you need to retain their engagement. In other words, you need to keep them reading. Lastly, you need to make them take action.

On Facebook, a user can only perform a few actions that can benefit your client; these are liking, sharing, and clicking on links. If your copy has made the target users take favorable actions, then you have done your part as a copywriter.

Liking

A "like" is Facebook's version of an up-vote. It has two purposes. First, it increases the reach of a post. As people like your post, it may also be shown on their friends' newsfeeds. The posts that were liked by friends will show in either on your newsfeed or in your notifications box when you click on the bell in the upper right side of the newsfeed page.

The second function of a like is as a subscribe button for pages. The posts on a liked page will appear in the person's newsfeed. This will increase the probability that future posts will have better engagement because more people will see them.

Sharing

Sharing, on the other hand, is the feature that will make your posts become viral. When people share your content, it will appear in their timeline as well as in their friends' newsfeeds.

Clicking on links

If you promise your clients that you can make a lot of users click on their post links on Facebook, then you will have a considerable edge against your content marketing competitors. This task, however, is not easy to do because people don't easily click on links.

There are generally two ways to get clicks, likes, and shares: through organic Facebook marketing and paid advertisements. Your role as a copywriter is to increase the likelihood that people will like and share content in organic or paid marketing.

You can do this by following these tips:

Appeal to people's emotions

People on Facebook are there to have a good time. They spend so much time on Facebook because posts remind them of people they have met and things that they have experienced in the past. That is why posts for things like "Throwback Thursday" persist until now. To make them like or share a post of a page, you should use emotional topics in your copies.

Use your target user's language and way of speaking

When posting, you could appeal better to a specific market if you talk the way they do. If you are targeting engineers, for example, then you should also use jargon and technical terms that only they will understand. If you are targeting a specific nationality, you may become more successful if you post status updates and links that speak their language.

Use words popular on the internet

Some words are more magnetic to people on the internet than others. For instance, the word 'awesome' is a great word to use regularly if you are targeting users in their teens and early adulthood. Other magnetic words are: "Wow", "Never", "Inspiring", "Die or Dead", "Definitely", "Feel", "Terrified", and "Amazing." (seems like an odd list)

In the past, words like "Free", "Now", and "You" were eye-catchers but many internet users have now associated them to annoying ads and pop-ups. You should expect the same phenomenon to happen with any attention-grabbing words on Facebook. People will eventually learn to ignore them when they become too popular.

Use the "post description" to catch attention

The post or ad description is the first thing that users read after your page name. If that part is not interesting, then they will move on to the next item on their newsfeed. You should use this to gain attention and create curiosity by adding more powerful words. For instance, popular pages use "this", "that" and similar pronouns often. Here are some examples:

"This man can't believe what he was seeing"

"That's not right. This shouldn't be legal."

Adding a picture that matches the description will also increase the likelihood of a like, a share, or a click.

Use the power of the red arrow in photos.

One of the most effective combinations when making people click on links is by using the powerful pronouns suggested above and adding a photo that has a red arrow to refer to the thing or person being represented by the pronoun. For instance, if your headline goes something like this: (missing headline?)

You should also add a photo of a person driving while texting and an arrow pointing at the driver. This will not only grab the attention of the users but also make them curious as to what will happen to the driver.

The end... almost!

Reviews are not easy to come by.

As an independent author with a tiny marketing budget, I rely on readers, like you, to leave a short review on Amazon.

Even if it's just a sentence or two!

So if you enjoyed the book, please...

\>\> Click here to leave a brief review on Amazon.

https://www.amazon.com/review/create-review?asin=XXXXXXXXX

I am very appreciative for your review as it truly makes a difference.

Thank you from the bottom of my heart for purchasing this book and reading it to the end.

Conclusion

"The competitor to be feared is one who never bothers about you at all, but goes on making his own business better all the time."

– Henry Ford

Despite the overview of this book, you must take it further if you want to become the best copywriter you can. Throughout the book, the tips that were given were to help you to see that content marketing isn't just about writing an elaborate description of a product. It's about convincing a target audience they can't live without having a certain product. It's about their belief in the product. It's also about being able to express all of this in such a way that your message targets the audience most likely to buy the product you are selling.

Look into the competition and find their weaknesses. The iPad advertisers did this perfectly, in that they knew the public still suspiciously views the innovative and complicated systems produced by iPad competitors. Instead of describing their system in a really complex manner, they demonstrated it as totally suitable to everyone's lifestyle in a stylish way. That is clever, honest content marketing and it hits the target audience in a way no one could have anticipated. The new iPad Air has equally taken the imagination of the public by storm by offering a lightweight the old iPad didn't offer. You'd be hard-pressed to make an iPad user part with the technology once you made the sale.

We told a similar story about cut-price airlines and how luxury airlines exploited the fact that "no frills" may not be what a discerning traveler is looking for. A good copywriter knows the following:

- The benefits of the product to target population
- The competition and what it offers in comparison with your product
- The medium by which advertising will be spread
- The time limits or constraints the copywriter must work within
- The public sector at which the adverts are aimed

Once you add the wonders of great vocabulary and come up with a brief but imaginative copy people automatically associate with the product, you will have sufficient information to persuade the public to buy your product. Look back at the catchphrases we shared with you, as some of these are extremely typical of what is being used to lure the public in these days. Some of these will last for generations as consumers believe in what they are investing.

You are selling a brand. Think Nike and the catchphrase that instantly comes to mind is, "Just Do It." If that doesn't push people who are having trouble making up their minds, then nothing will. Brands depend upon copywriters to come up with the right copy to sell, and the examples shown to you in this book are first-rate examples.

Disneyland is still selling tickets based on the fact that it's purported to be "the happiest place on Earth." This appeals to both grown-ups and kids alike, who are seeking out an adventure that takes them away from the doldrums of normalcy and into another world where people are all happy.

All of this is a lot for one person to work on, but it's all part and parcel of working as a copywriter. If you feel you have the imagination and can play with words to pass on a message, then perhaps this is the career for you. With a Bachelor's Degree in Advertising, followed by or during which freelance work is undertaken, you stand a good chance to become one of the best. Keep up to date with current trends, and you will find the work is rewarding as you experience success.

Freelance work is always available, though if you wish to have the security of being employed by an advertising company or a public relations company, this should be your goal. Online companies are offering jobs to copywriters, but be aware you may lose copyright of written work, as clients paying for work tend to take that as part of the deal. Mind you, that's not much different to working for an agency because the agency takes copyright on what their employees produce. If you are happy with that, you can think of this as being a practice run to actually working in an advertising environment with the agency taking all of the credit for the work you produce.

It's a very satisfying career and one that suits people who are not afraid of new things. It would also suit those who are open to changes and working for different clients with different needs. Specializing in a field is also possible, such as cosmetics, industry, etc., and your specialist area could also be backed up by qualifications that show your knowledge of the product range. However, never close the entrance door to opportunity. The best content marketing I ever did was on a product I knew nothing about before undergoing all of the investigation needed to be able to produce. The fact that the product was new to me opened up new avenues of exploration, and perhaps it was the freshness of approach that made it such a success.

I wish you well in content marketing. You may have decided by now content marketing isn't for you. You may not want your writing associated with branding or product sales, but for those who do, this is a rewarding career move that gives a steady flow of work and great pay. You may not earn millions, but you will never know until you try. It's enjoyable, for every job taken is different, and you change your approach every time you have a new copy to write. Otherwise, you get stale. If you are stuck in your ways as a writer, you can't expect to pitch like a pro, which is what content marketing is all about.

Content marketing takes your writing skills one step further than straight writing. Does that mean that you can't have heroes and heroines? Of course not. You only have to see the adverts on the television screen to know that even advertising copy allows you the benefit of creativity. Think of all the memorable advertisements you have ever seen and know that behind every one of them was a very clever copywriter who somehow got it right. If you can remember the advert, they did their job properly. That's what you need to be aiming for.

The adverts that stand out in your mind or the copy you read on the Internet that struck a chord with you is clever content marketing. This book has many exercises and you will be able to go through them time and time again, choosing different products and objects to use. It pays to work on items you find boring as well as those that you find exciting because a good copywriter can make even the mundane sound necessary and exciting to the buying public. If you have spare time, pick up an object and try to describe it using all of the styles relevant to content marketing - all of the practice you get helps you to be able to change styles instantly to suit the market and the age range to who you are aiming your copy. Often, bad content marketing shows up big time, which allows you to keep working within the parameters set by your client without making you look foolish or as if you have not understood the brief you have been given.

DOWNLOAD YOUR FREE GIFT BELOW:

These 14 New Habits Will Double Your Income, from Today

An Easy Cheat Sheet to Adopting 14 Powerful Success Habits:

Stop Procrastinating and Start Earning with Intent Now!

Are Your Bad Habits Keeping You from the Life You Want?

Mine definitely were, but then I dedicated myself to *new habits* – and everything changed!

Most people get stuck in same old routines. We eat the same breakfast, we talk to the same people. Human beings are creatures of habit, and it locks us into negative cycles we don't even know are there.

Like me, you've had enough of the same-old, same-old. It's time for change!

This guide gives you the 14 most high impact habits that helped me double my income nearly instantly, when I set out on this journey. I will help you change, and I'll make it stick!

This FREE Cheat Sheet contains:

- Daily success habits that the most successful people in the world live by

- Common, but little-known habits that will surprise you

- Details on what Stephen Covey, Oprah Winfrey, Elon Musk, Bill Gates and Albert Einstein did that you aren't doing to maximize your earning potential

- Tips on how to overcome habit fatigue

- The reality of adopting difficult, challenging habits and the rewards that result

Scroll below and <u>click the link to claim</u> your cheat sheet!

It's tough to admit that you're doing it wrong. I went through it, and it sucks. After that I was free to change however necessary, to meet my goals. I want you to know that change is waiting for you. This guide is so easy to follow, and if you put it to work in your life – you will double your income.

Adopt these habits, and change your life.

CLICK HERE!!

Check Out Our Other AMAZING Titles:

Book 1: Social Media Marketing 2020

The Ultimate Guide to Boosting Your Business Through Social Media Marketing Efforts

Developing a Working Social Media Marketing Strategy

Content Marketing

"The essence of strategy is choosing what not to do."

- Michael Porter

The easiest way to flop at marketing your business over social media is by rushing into it without having a solid plan or a working strategy. Sadly, this is what happens to most entrepreneurs and business owners. It could also happen to you. You can start a Facebook business page without knowing why you need it. What's worse is that you don't learn how you would measure if it is successful or not.

So, where should you start when developing a social media marketing strategy? This is the question that most business owners seek answers to.

The best place of beginning your social media marketing strategy is understanding the meaning of social media. You should get to know what it is and what it is not. Social media is not the run in the mill form of advertising or marketing. Social media entails the combination of technology with social interaction through sharing of images, videos, and words. In a nutshell, social media refers to "conversations" made convenient and richer.

Part of the strategy also includes listening to your customers, projections, and rivals in the same industry. Get to understand what your competitors are doing on social media. What are the customers saying about the products and services being offered? Is there a gap that needs to be filled? Analyzing what customers are saying is an excellent way of getting to know them. The good news is that information can be attained by simply listening to conversations over social media. As a business owner, it would be your work to help your clients find answers to their queries. If possible rely on analytical tools which could range from basic tools such as Google Alerts to sophisticated tools such as Radian6.

Auditing Your Online Presence on Social Media Channels

Having understood the importance of a working plan when developing a social media marketing strategy, it is worth taking a look at the social media audit. Basically, this is a follow-up. What you are doing is that you are following up on the strategy that you are using to market your brand over social media.

What is a social media audit? It refers to the process whereby you take time to review what is working and what is not working in your strategy. Also, the process entails examining the areas that can be enhanced to guarantee the best results. It is quite likely that you think that the process would be challenging. Well, it isn't. Numerous social media analytic tools are at your disposal. With the help of these tools, the auditing process would be straightforward.

The main issue here is; how do you go about auditing your online presence on social media. A key step to take would be to review all social channels that your business is associated with. Take time to go through all the social channels without bias. Often, business owners would overlook other social channels since they are not popular. Whether you are running a popular social channel or a YouTube channel with only 20 subscribers, you have to consider them with equal importance.

Next, it is time to decide where you want to focus on depending on the product that you are dealing with. Here, most people would go for the top four social media channels such as Facebook, Twitter,

Content Marketing

LinkedIn, and Instagram. I cannot entirely say that focusing on a particular channel would not work. However, it is advisable to try as much as possible to invest in these channels equally. Bear in mind that their marketing returns would differ. Hence, it is never wise to put all your eggs in one basket.

Recording information is part of the social media auditing process. Here, you are required to record what you have found out regarding your analysis of the social channels that your business is linked with. Record the number of followers for each platform. Take note of the frequency of visits to the respective pages. How quickly do people respond to your posts over these platforms? Do you notice any changes with increasing posts from your end? These crucial facts will help you in gauging what works and what doesn't for your business.

As you scheme through your social media pages, it is essential that you check for consistency. Your brand should be represented in a way that it is not confusing to the audience. Consequently, if there is a website where you have slightly changed the logo, you should correct this with immediate effect. Ensure that you are keen on the colors that you use to guarantee consistency. Visitors accessing your videos on Instagram should have a similar perception when they access these videos on Facebook and LinkedIn.

Also, posts made on different social media sites should be compatible with the platforms in question. YouTube, for example, is a great place to post long videos. Shorter videos should be posted to other platforms such as Twitter, Facebook, or Instagram. Most importantly, unique content would appeal to your audience. For that reason, it is worth investing your money in creating innovative and engaging content for your audience to enjoy.

Social media auditing demands that you take the time to evaluate how your audience is interacting with the content you posted. One fact is that different social media pages will host various kinds of people. Take a look at Pinterest, for example. The platform has got more women as compared to men. In fact, over 70% of its users are women.

On the contrary, when you look at Google Plus, most users are men. So, before posting content over the different social pages, it is worth mulling over the content. Ask yourself if you are posting the right content to the right platform? A careful analysis of the content interaction with the market will aid in understanding your viewers better. Ultimately, you will end up posting relevant and engaging content which transforms into promising sales leads.

After auditing all your profiles for consistency and evaluating the content that you are posting, the next thing is to look forward. Decide on what is essential for your business growth over the coming few months. Set small yet achievable goals. One of your short-term goals could be increasing your followers or increasing the number of responses for a certain percentage. The results of your social media auditing should be saved for future reference.

Know Your Customers' Tastes and Preferences

Knowing your customers' tastes and preferences is key to any business success. This is because customers are the main determinants of the success of a business. After all, they are the source of business profits. Therefore, they are regarded as the most fundamental element of any business. Most companies that thrive in their market of operation often fulfill the promises that they make to their clients. However, meeting customer needs first requires that you understand them. It is imperative that a business owner should understand the customers to the extent that they can easily anticipate their needs and after that deliver beyond expectations.

Understanding customer tastes and preferences does not necessarily mean that one should engage with them on a personal level. Instead, it entails customer segmentation. Different customers would require different products and services. Therefore, a business owner could get to know his customers by coming up with focus groups. For example, if you are selling baby clothes, your target group would be mothers or rather parents having small kids. Developing focus groups requires that you segment your market based on gender, age, occupation, and disposable income. Doing this guarantees that you serve them better.

Customer shopping habits is another way of understanding them from a different perspective. What are some of the shopping trends that can be associated with your target market? Such shopping trends could be identified through the "Likes" and "Retweets" that your customers are posting or sharing. Certainly, if more customers like a specific product over social media, this means that they are looking to purchase it. Hence, a good move would be offering a discount coupon for that product over social media.

Similarly, shopping habits could be identified through customers' conversations. Often, people would want their friends to own products that work. Therefore, it is not surprising to find people frequently conversing that a particular brand is better than the other. This is where your business comes in. Understanding their tastes and preferences ensures that you are a step ahead of them. Before they know it, your social media page would be suggesting to them why your product suits their needs.

An important thing that companies should bear in mind is that they should find the best social media channel that suits them. Just because a rival brand is using Facebook to market its products does not mean that it would also work for you. You might end up making a terrible mistake by following the wind. Settling for an appropriate social channel is another way of getting to know your customers better. A business that deals with lady products would work best if it promotes its products over Pinterest as compared to Google Plus. It is because there are more women on Pinterest as compared to Google Plus. Hence, understanding your customers also demands that you choose the right channel to reach them.

Today, there are hundreds of brands in the market that are suffering as they failed to get personal with their customers. Getting to know your customers on a personal level is key to ensuring that your social media presence works to your advantage. When using social media to market products and services, business owners should understand that these platforms are there to bring them closer to their clients. Therefore, it is imperative to build long-lasting relationships with individuals over social media. Unfortunately, some businesses overlook this need. They ignore customer complaints posted on social media platforms. Some of them even send rude responses to clients forgetting that the success of the business depends on them. It is worth noting that minor issues can be escalated to the point of tarnishing a business' image. Consequently, companies are consistently advised to seek to build a personal relationship with their clients over social media pages that they are associated with.

Engaged customers on social media would defend a brand that they are loyal to. A business should consider these customers as their advocates. They are the individuals to convince other people regardless of the complaints that are being posted about your product or service. As such, it is good that businesses recognize this group of shoppers and reward them accordingly.

A marketing expert would not forget to mention the importance of constant engagement with customers over social media. Socialites are always out hunting for information. They want to be ahead of others in relation to products and services that they might be using. For that reason, work to give them what they need. Engage with them by continually informing them that there are new products set to be launched. Make your followers work as your brand ambassadors. If your pitch is excellent, you can expect good results.

A Mission Statement That Defines Your Brand

If you have been keen on the internet, you should have noticed that almost all businesses have mission statements. Why are these mission statements significant? In short, a mission statement is a statement that helps a company to remain focused on its goals. Your mission statement will, therefore, keep your head focused on the marketing goal that you have on social media.

Besides the social media strategy that you have in mind, having a mission statement is vital. Yes, you have all those goals on how you will increase your audience by a certain percentage or how you would boost your engagement. But you also need to have a target. An archer will never shoot blindly without having a goal to aim. The main idea here is that you need to have a sense of direction.

Don't fall into the trap where most business owners waste their time and money on social media just because it is a cheaper form of marketing. Cheap is expensive. You should have known that by know. Make use of social media as a marketing tool because you understand that it is an essential tool for achieving your business goals. So, a mission statement will act as a roadmap to guaranteeing that your social media use is a success.

Your mission statement should answer the specific results that you want or anticipate for your business now that you plan to use social media as a marketing tool. Also, an appropriate mission statement should detail where you will be focusing your efforts on the marketing campaign. And most of all, it should outline the primary reason as to why you opted to use social media as an ideal choice for your marketing demands.

Book 2: Learn How to Become a Self-Publisher From A Self Published Millionaire

Scale Your Way to a Passive Six Figure Income

I had mentioned earlier that you could choose to write your own books, but this would be a less than optimal use of your time despite the savings it provides. This chapter is going to show you why the reason behind it and why you need to think like a publisher and not an author.

There are a whole host of other things you need to set up to release your book and prepare it for a successful launch. You will learn all about that in this chapter.

Production

The first step to producing your book is to narrow down the formats you wish to create. You can offer three formats to your customers: eBook, paperback, and audiobook. Audiobooks, understandably, require different production methods from the other two, and I'll discuss this in more detail in another chapter.

Whatever you choose to publish a book, the first step is to write it or have it written. Given that you will be releasing multiple books per month, you need to ask yourself whether you can actually write these many books within that time. Conservatively, you will need to release four books per month.

Each book will need to be at least thirty thousand words or else you risk receiving extremely negative reviews, criticizing your books as being 'pamphlets' and not actual books. In the earlier days of KDP, you could get away with publishing a garbage 1000 word article and calling it a book, but these days doing such things will lead to an account suspension from Amazon.

Besides, producing good quality books is just good business. This should be self-explanatory. Unless you're a speedy writer and are knowledgeable about the topics on hand, you can realistically produce this level of output. However, this is unlikely to happen. Thus, you need to hire a ghostwriter.

The World of Ghostwriting

Ghostwriting is something that happens all the time in the literary world. The articles you read in magazines and trade publications that are purportedly written by a CEO or industry leader have actually been written by a ghostwriter. The ghostwriter and the CEO work together to determine what themes ought to be expressed and the writer simply puts words to them.

Many of the autobiographies of celebrities are ghostwritten. It's a bit odd to expect people to have excellent writing and storytelling skills, no matter how skilled they might be in other areas of life. Hiring a ghostwriter is a good decision and is a great investment for your business.

When you hire a ghostwriter, you will need to sign a contract with them that stipulates all the rights to the work will belong to you and that they are not entitled to receive any royalties or credit from the sale of the book. This is a pretty standard contract that you can draft via a template searched on Google. So where should you hire a ghostwriter?

The most obvious places are on freelancer sites such as Upwork or Fiverr. Upwork is the most popular freelance site for slightly pricier assignments whereas Fiverr tends to be cheaper. You might be tempted to go cheap and hire the person who quotes the lowest rate, but remember that your book is an asset for your business and this is practically your face to your customers.

You need to invest in the quality of the book. That being said, how much should you invest? Well, usually paying $1.50 per 100 words is considered a good rate. You're still paying around one cent per word, so a 30,000-word book will cost you around $450. However, when hiring a writer there are a number of things you need to consider.

The first is the quality of the writer. Upwork is particularly notorious for this with a number of fake profiles pervading that site despite having to pay to use their services. Generally speaking, it is extremely difficult to either be a writer on that website or find a good writer, so everyone loses. Fiverr is geared toward graphic design and more, shall we say, eccentric tasks so it is unlikely you will find a good writer there.

Beyond quality, you also need to worry about editing and proofreading the copy. As I said, you cannot get away with poorly edited copy and you can bet that your readers will make themselves heard if this is the case. It is extremely annoying to read a piece of text that is misspelled or has poor grammar, so it is in your interest to have this done to your manuscript.

You also need to take care that the document is properly formatted. eBooks and paperbacks require different formatting requirements, which can be painful to do yourself. While the tasks you need to do are simple in and of themselves, doing them over and over again can become annoying or frustrating.

There is also the possibility of fraud. The first level of fraud to watch out for is the old college trick of using invisible characters to beef up the word count. Upwork's writers are notorious for this sort of nonsense. Secondly, there is a far more serious problem to take care of: plagiarism.

Make no mistakes; publishing a plagiarized book and indicating that you hold the rights to it is a straight road to an account ban. Your account will not be reinstated so you can kiss your business goodbye before it even begins.

The best solution is to use a ghostwriting company. Companies such as The Urban Writers have excellent writers on board and do the vetting process for you, along with the editing, proofreading and plagiarism scan. The downside is that you will pay more for this comfort. Generally, you will need to pay $2.90 per 100 words, which works out to $870 per 30,000-word book.

It is this number that I referred to earlier that you will need to spend $1000 per book. Remember, you get what you pay for. If you're comfortable hiring a freelancer yourself, go for it. Remember that there will be some false steps and that your chosen freelancer will not always be available. In the end, you can either spend your time chasing people around endlessly or pay for the comfort of not doing that.

A final word on this. A lot of self-proclaimed 'indie' authors disparage the use of ghostwriting companies and refer to publishers who do this as somehow being "fake." These "artists" invariably fail to sell any books, so you can guess where the vitriol is coming from. If ghostwriting is good enough for a busy CEO, it ought to be good enough for your purposes as well.

Covers and Formatting

The quality of your book is important, but the most important thing for your success is the quality of your covers. Your cover is like the headline of an article you've written. It needs to draw people in and get them to click on your book. If you have excellent photoshop skills, you can design the covers yourself. Your image quality needs to be over 300 dpi, remember.

For the rest of us, we can safely use Fiverr to hire a freelancer to design a great cover. Mind you, there are two kinds of covers you will need. One is an eBook cover and the other is a paperback cover. The paperback cover needs to take into account the page count of your paperback manuscript, so until you've finished formatting it, don't order the paperback cover.

Amazon allows you to use any number of pen names you want so you don't have to use your own name to publish. Once you receive your manuscript from your ghostwriter, you need to first make sure it is formatted for Kindle. This is as simple as inserting a page break after every chapter and making sure the headings of the chapters are formatted according to the heading 1,2, and 3 formats.

Paperback formatting is trickier. You first need to choose the trim size of your book. The most popular paperback size is 6X9 inches; however, KDP allows you to print in different sizes. Now you have to decide whether the page needs to be white or cream. Cream paper is thicker and this affects the paperback cover's spine size.

You can hire a freelancer to format this for you, or you can do it yourself. Personally, I do it myself. You can Google "formatting guide for KDP paperback" and so on to receive step by step instructions. If you're planning to hire someone, don't pay more than $10 to do this, since it really isn't that difficult unless you have some special requirements. The same applies to the book cover as well, but if you feel the need to invest more into it, do so.

Once your manuscript is formatted, note the trim size and page count and hire a freelancer to convert your eBook cover into paperback. If you're proficient in Photoshop, you can do this yourself. KDP provides the trim size templates and the guidelines as well. You will need to create the spine and the back cover as layers and make sure that the book's title is on the spine.

That's all there is to it.

Description and Backend Keywords

Content Marketing

Your book's product page needs a description. When uploading your book on the KDP backend, you can write a description there. Unfortunately, that area on the backend doesn't allow you to add HTML tags to highlight or create a bulleted list. It is simply a text box.

Your description is what is going to sell your book, so you need to devote some time to this. You can hire a copywriter to do this for you. However, there's still the question of formatting. To do this, head over to the Kindlepreneur website and search for the book description generator. This will generate HTML tags which you can paste into KDP.

Next, you need to find keywords to create a keyword cloud for your book. KDP gives you seven boxes and people make the mistake of thinking you can use just seven keywords. This is absolutely not the case. You can stuff your keywords into these boxes and the algorithm still considers them as valid.

Where do you find additional, relevant keywords? The first place to use is the Amazon search bar. You don't need to stick to just the suggestions that come up when you search for your keyword. Instead, use related terms to your keyword and use those suggestions as well. Google suggestions are a good source for these as well.

Now that your keywords and covers are all lined up, it is time to set up your ARC team.

ARC Teams

Despite the catchy name, ARC stands for advance review copy. This team is a group of reviewers who you will send your book in advance of your release so that they can provide you with reviews, ideally to boost the enthusiasm about the book's launch.

If you already have a blog of some kind or a distribution channel on the web, you probably don't need any advice on how to build a team. It is as simple as having people sign up for your newsletter and providing them with a free copy and instructing them to mention this fact in their review once the book launches.

First-time publishers without any such access are at a disadvantage here. It is better to start building your ARC team while your book is being written. The best way of doing this is to search Facebook groups dedicated to this. Genres of all kinds have FB groups and you can set up a landing page where people can sign up to your email list.

Another great option is to use Booksprout, which is free for up to 20 reviewers. After that, you will need to pay, but this is a good investment. Some slightly more expensive services are ExclusiveARC and Hidden Gems Books. Goodreads is a great place to network with book bloggers and people interested in your genre. As a first time publisher, you will need to establish some credibility, but it is well worth it.

Lastly, insert a link to signup for your newsletter in the first few pages of your book. This way, you can continue to build your ARC team as your book sales grow. Building the first few members of your team is the toughest task, but it gets easier as you publish your books and gain credibility.

Remember to give your ARC team at least three weeks to read and instruct them to leave a feedback within 14 days of your book's launch. When launching your book, enroll it in KDP select and run a free promotion for the first five days. This will help build a buzz and will get you additional reviews. Once the promotion ends, price it appropriately in line with the rest of your competition and you'll be all set.

Monitor the reviews of those in your ARC and remove those who are not contributing reviews. You can engage them and check whether there are any issues but if this persists over time, don't hesitate to cut them out of your group.

As a final word: there are services that guarantee five-star reviews and make promises as to the number of reviews you will receive. Understand that these are black hat tactics and Amazon takes a dim view of such manipulation. This is against TOS and you'll end up in all sorts of trouble. Hence, don't do it. Make sure you're not buying reviews in any way.

Paying a service to promote your book is perfectly fine, though.

A note on all of this: if you're publishing no or low content books, you don't need an ARC team. Neither do you need to do too much to produce your book. Use PowerPoint to create lined pages and save them as a PDF. Set up your keywords on the backend correctly and stuff your title with relevant keywords. Once this is done, use AMS ads to promote your book. I'll discuss this in detail in a later chapter.

Book Setup and Upload

Uploading your book onto KDP's dashboard is quite straightforward. Take care to enable DRM for your ebook, which gives you full rights to the content and allow lending and signup for Kindle matchbook using the "free" option. This drives sales so it's important that you opt for these.

Go for KDP select initially but once your free promotion is over, opt out of it by emailing KDP and requesting them to remove your book. This only prevents you from running the five-day free promos in the future. The royalty situation has been explained previously and as such, doesn't really affect you.

Paperbacks have an additional wrinkle in that you need to choose whether you want KDP to provide you with an ISBN or you want to use your own. In the United States, you need to pay around $750 for 100 ISBNs and $125 for one. You can buy one from Bowker or Nielsen on the web.

If you choose to publish your book on another platform, you will need a separate ISBN. While this is perfectly acceptable to do, it is considered extremely unprofessional in the book-buying world. Thus, if your aim is to have Barnes and Noble or libraries carry your book, you might want to invest in an ISBN. My advice? Don't buy ISBNs for nonfiction and buy them for fiction books. Don't bother for low or no content books and stick to the free option since you'll be publishing on KDP only.

Set your paperback price to at least $16.99 and play around with the prices in euros and pounds as you wish. In the case of eBooks, choose the price that is in line with the rest of the books in the search results.

Hit publish and you're done!

Book 3: Building a Massive Social Following

Build your Brand's Following using Leading Strategies and Tips

Blogs - Your Social Media Centre

"We don't have a choice on whether we do social media, the question is how well we do it."

– Erik Qualman

When it comes to building a massive social media following, the role that blogs play should not be discounted. There are numerous blogs in existence today, and people refer to blogs for almost half of the questions they have. This means, with a great blog, you can quickly amass a considerable amount of relevant following, so long as you post relevant content. In this chapter, we will be looking into blogs and why they are essential to your brand.

Blogs: What Are They?

A blog, in its purest form, can be defined as a vehicle where individuals can clearly express their thoughts using whatever medium they deem fit. The internet, since its inception, has been transformed from a directory into a digital wellspring of information and knowledge, and bloggers were able to take full advantage of that. If you were to stop anybody on the street and ask them what their first port of call for getting their questions answered was, they would point towards the internet.

The internet is also a medium in which people can gain more information about their world. For this reason, blogging has to be an essential part of any brand's social media strategy. For businesses, regardless of size, a blog offers the opportunity to provide more information concerning products, services, promos, advertisements, and more while also providing an avenue for customers to get answers to their questions.

How Does a Blog Help Your Brand?

For businesses that are concerned about increasing their brand visibility, blogging offers an opportunity to put the brand at the forefront of prospective customers' minds. A blog lets businesses show customers that their needs and wants are acknowledged; it also provides information for a brand's target audience to make an informed decision when choosing to conduct business with the brand.

Given its simple, early days, it can be easy to discount blogging as writing on a page, but there is a lot more to it. Blogging about relevant content that readers can either connect with or gain value from is the primary purpose of having a blog on your website. There are numerous types of blog content, each with their own benefits; however, your blog mustn't become saturated with sell pieces. These types of content typically aim to sell a service or a product to the reader, and while it does have its place in the blogging sphere, when misused, it can decrease the number of recurring visitors to your blog, thereby harming your brand, and of course your following.

Blogging, as part of a social media campaign, takes content creation a step further. This type of blog aims to get people to see a much more insightful part of you or your brand than what is available on social media. The persona they see on social media should be reflected in the blogs only more in-depth. As with all social media platforms, you must pay attention to metrics to know how much traffic your blog is getting, as well as create a comments section that enables readers to put out their thoughts and feelings.

This comment section should not be taken lightly by any brand as it offers a wonderful treasure trove of honest opinions concerning your brand and the topic at large. You should also do your part by interacting with visitors in the comments section by replying and posing answers and rebuttals to their comments. Doing this ensures that there is a healthy dialogue between your brand and your prospective customers.

While it can be said that blogging is a marketing tool, it should be viewed more like an insight or analytical tool in the sense that you can impart information to your target audience and they can provide honest feedback to you concerning your efforts. When a blog site is combined with other social media tools such as Facebook, Instagram,

LinkedIn, and Twitter, you can grow your brand's online visibility and your customer base at the same time.

Perhaps a decade ago, it would have been unfathomable to consider linking social media and blogging together. Blogging was seen as the antithesis of social media, in the sense that social media was instantaneous, somewhat personal, and of course, a short-form of media, while blogging was touted to be serious, professional, and a more detail-oriented format. Given that they are so different, experts postulated that blogging would die out after being replaced by social media, due to the ever-decreasing attention span of the public. This train of thought is false. What experts did not take into account was the fact that the content used in blogging and social media are nearly the same. The same in the sense that a brand could highlight a topic on a social media platform like Twitter and push its followers that are interested in getting a deeper understanding of the topic to its blog.

When operating a blog, there are certain things you must pay attention to. The first is to have content that is relevant to your brand and insightful. Your blog content should be value-packed and high quality so that your posts can be shared and re-shared. It should also meet the need of your followers. If visitors see that their needs are being met, they are more inclined to share your content, thereby increasing your visibility.

Just because it is a blog does not mean it should only contain writing. Your posts have to be visually stimulating. You can add a video or a picture. This is especially true for blog posts that are paired to posts on social media. These types of posts should have content that either informs, analyses, or answers questions.

It is one thing to have a blog and have a social media account, and it is another to actively link the two together, so there is no segmentation when it comes to your followers. A way to do this is to employ the use of share buttons. Share buttons let visitors to your blog site seamlessly share your content on the social media platform of their choosing.

Blogs as Your Social Media Center

If you remember, at the beginning of the chapter, it was stated that blogs and social media have a symbiotic relationship. If you want to build a massive social media following, you have to ensure that your blog is the center of your social media. What this means is that your social media accounts should be linked to your blogs. You have to create an avenue for people to seamlessly follow you on social media. This involves adding links to your social media accounts, which people can follow once they deem the content on your blog to be relevant to them.

There are times when people see certain articles and wish they could save to read for a later time, but they are unable to. What then happens is that they give up on that article, and the writer of that article has lost not only a reader, but a potential subscriber or follower. This is something that you must ensure does not happen to your content, and that's where a "Pin for Later" feature comes in. Having this on your blog ensures that people can save articles for a later date, and they are also reminded of engaging with you and your content.

To direct traffic to your blog and by extension, your social media accounts, you must make use of email lists. Email lists might appear to be archaic in today's social media climate; however, they are still beneficial as a marketing tool. Look at it this way, people can decide to follow you on social media and never engage your content at all, but if they sign up for a mailing list, they have taken the proactive step to be inundated with your content. They are also more likely to read the contents of your email and then proceed to follow you on social media, to get a real-time update on the topics you are a subject matter expert on.

When creating emails for your email lists, it is imperative that you make it as attractive as possible. You can make use of imagery by adding graphics to your email. When adding graphics, you should follow the philosophy of "less is more." Having too many graphics in your email can make your email come across as spam or junk mail to the reader. You should have an excellent subject line that can seamlessly grab the attention of your readers. When creating an email, it can be so easy to begin rambling and end up with more content than is deemed necessary. Your email should be short, and it should contain information that is relevant to the reader.

When it comes to listing out social media networks, a forgotten platform is LinkedIn. Most people do not view LinkedIn as a social media platform; they see it as a job site or a business development site. There is so much more to LinkedIn than meets the eye. Think about it from a brand's perspective; there are millions of people being active on LinkedIn, using it to better their career or business prospects. If you are a brand that sees the viability of such a target audience, it would be foolhardy not to take advantage of it. You can be sure that every individual on the site is who they say they are. LinkedIn and blogging seem to be like a perfect marriage, as LinkedIn enables you as either a brand or an individual to post long-form content on subjects that are based around your online brand and on the subject matter you are an expert on.

However, in addition to blogs and LinkedIn, another platform that is just as important is Twitter. The next chapter will be looking into this platform and the array of benefits it offers.

www.ingramcontent.com/pod-product-compliance
Lightning Source LLC
Chambersburg PA
CBHW021824170526
45157CB00007B/2681